Olmecs

A Captivating Guide to the Earliest Known Major Ancient Civilization in Mexico

Free Bonus from Captivating History (Available for a Limited time)

Hi History Lovers!

Now you have a chance to join our exclusive history list so you can get your first history ebook for free as well as discounts and a potential to get more history books for free! Simply visit the link below to join.

Captivatinghistory.com/ebook

Also, make sure to follow us on:

Twitter: @Captivhistory

Facebook: Captivating History:@captivatinghistory

Contents

Introduction

When most people think about pre-Columbian Mesoamerica, they often jump straight to Aztecs and Mayans, arguably the most famous and well-known native civilizations of this region. Of course, they are not to blame as historians themselves give those cultures most of their attention. This often leads to misconceptions about how civilized life actually began in the Americas. Some people think that civilization didn't exist in North America until the Europeans arrived; others think it all began with the Mayans.

In reality, the first people that managed to elevate themselves to civilized life were the Olmecs. They remain relatively unknown, hidden in the long and dark corridors of forgotten history. Most of their culture remains wrapped in mystery, which may explain why so few historians are ready to tackle the task of uncovering the true story of the Olmecs. It is a difficult job, and even after many decades devoted to researching Olmecs, answers may not show up. And usually, with every answer, a new question arises. In a way, it's a Sisyphean task. Because there aren't written sources and histories of the Olmecs, their exact story remains unknown. And most of our knowledge about them are just theories based on archeological findings.

So, anyone brave enough to take on the task of learning about the Olmecs should be prepared for a lot of ifs, maybes, probabilities, and likelihoods, not to mention the conflicted opinions of various historians. With all that in mind, one could get discouraged from even trying. But, as the earliest known civilization in America, they deserve some of our attention. Their tale deserves to be told.

Chapter 1 – Who Were the Olmecs?

The most honest answer you'll get for this question is "We are not exactly sure." These people, known as the Olmecs, occupied southcentral parts of present-day Mexico, in what are today states of Veracruz and Tabasco, on the shores of the Gulf of Mexico. They emerged in these tropical lowlands somewhere around 1400 BCE and created what is considered one of the first civilizations in Mesoamerica. For roughly one thousand years, they were the most developed and most powerful nation in this area. During that time they dominated the region through trade and military might, spreading their more sophisticated culture and civilization to neighboring tribes. And then around 400 BCE, just as suddenly as they arrived, they had disappeared into the thick Mexican jungles.

The Olmec heartland.

For almost two thousand years they were forgotten, but during the 19th century, as archeology began to expand and evolve into a serious science, historians started to notice a specific type of jade sculpture with jaguar-like features. It was a unique and powerful style that caught their attention. After some research, they found out that they came from the region we now know as the Olmec heartland, located along the Gulf coast. Early modern archeologists weren't sure how to name this new civilization, but one of them remembered that Aztecs from the 16th century CE told Spaniards about the people living in that area, who they called Olmeca (Ōlmēcah). In Aztecan Nahuatl language that means "rubber people". The name came from the widespread usage of rubber among the population of that region. Even though there is no real connection between the civilizations that in different times occupied the same territory, the name stuck. But we are almost certain that they didn't call themselves Olmeca.

It is worth mentioning that a poem in Nahuatl, recorded long after Europeans came to the Americas, tells a tale of a legendary land on the banks of "the eastern sea." In the poem, this mythical land, Tamoanchan, was settled long before the Aztecs founded their cities, in an era no one can remember. And its rule existed for a long time. What is even more intriguing about this poem is that the name Tamoanchan wasn't of Aztecan origins, but rather Mayan, the word Tamoanchan meaning "In the land of rain or mist." Some historians believe that the Olmecs heartland was described in the poem and that they actually spoke a variation of the Mayan language. But others disagree, claiming that the tongue of original Olmecs was actually an archaic form of Mixe–Zoquean language, which is still spoken in the area. Although the latter theory is now widely accepted, the truth is that due to the lack of archeological findings, we're still not certain about what exact language the Olmecs spoke.

After archeologist started to explore the Olmec sites more thoroughly during the early 20th century, they discovered many sites that could be linked with the so-called rubber people. But two of them stood out as the biggest and most important cities of the Olmecs. The first one was San Lorenzo, situated in the Coatzacoalcos River Basin. The first signs of human communities on that location are sometimes even dated way back to 1800 BCE. But those earliest settlements are usually considered to be pre-civilized societies. The actual rise of this city coincides with the rise of Olmec civilization itself, around 1400 BCE. But by 900 BCE, this site was mostly abandoned. The center of Olmec power and culture had moved by that time.

The second important Olmec archeological site is La Venta, located to the northeast of San Lorenzo in the swampy basin of the Tonalá river. It started to emerge around 1200 BCE, but after the fall of San Lorenzo, it took over as the center of the Olmec civilization. It stood as a bastion of the Olmecs, being home to some of their most important architectural creations. This city was abandoned around 400 BCE, which also marked the end of the Olmecs (at least in the way we think of them now). Of course, these weren't the only cities. There were many others, like Tres Zapotes, Laguna de Los Cerros, and El Manatí, but those never managed to match the wealth and power of San Lorenzo or La Venta. To avoid any misconceptions, it is important to note that these names aren't Olmecan names, but were given to the sites by the archeologists working on them in the unhospitable Mesoamerican jungles.

At first glance, even to the trained eye of an historian, the location of the Olmec heartland might seem a bit unwelcome for the start of a young civilization since it is located among the dense jungles and swamps with a humid climate. But when one takes into account that all major cities were located near rivers, which provided both fertile soil and easier travel, things start to make much more sense. And stepping back to see a wider geographical picture, we can notice that the Olmecs were located on an important trading route that connected regions which later spawned the Aztecs and Mayans. The location of the Olmecan civilization could be compared to other major civilizations, like the Sumerians in Mesopotamia, the Egyptians on the banks of the Nile, or the self-explanatory Indus Valley civilization. Combining those two essential elements explains why the earliest Mesoamerican civilization started right on that spot.

These few broad and vague details about the Olmecs given in this chapter only serve as an introduction to this civilization. Now it's time to dive deeper into the Olmec story, and like archeologists and historians, get a more explicit answer to the question posed in this chapter. And hopefully, by the end of this book, you'll have your own impression of who they were.

Chapter 2 – Emerging from the Jungle

Although it is not certain where the Olmecs actually came from, one shouldn't think that people just magically appeared in the Americas or that they evolved separately from humans on other continents. The currently accepted theory is that during the last Ice Age, somewhere between 30,000 and 10,000 years ago, the first humans came to North America. They crossed over a land bridge named Beringia that connected Alaska to the far eastern shores of present-day Russia. Another theory that is less accepted maintains that early settlers actually traveled by boats along the Pacific Coast. No matter which theory is closer to the truth, one thing is for certain—people slowly migrated south towards warmer climates and more fertile lands.

Around 8,000 BCE, due to the changes in temperature and sea level which came with the end of the Ice Age, early settlers in present-day Mexico started to change their lifestyle. They started to rely more on domesticated plants as their main source of food. Yet, their tribal organization remained on a rather basic level, more similar to how we see prehistorical humans. The next important step in the development of more complex lifestyle happened roughly around 2000 BCE. That is when an early village life started. It was a more organized way of living than before, a vital step in the development of civilized life in the Mesoamerican region since it brought growth in population and food surpluses, a necessity for the rise of more complex social and cultural life. Those crucial changes in society and way of life led to developments in the arts, as well as political and class stratification of most Mesoamerican societies.

At the same time, in similar circumstances like all others around them, the Olmecs started to build their civilization. In the beginning, around 1800-1700 BCE, they probably weren't much different than other tribes around them, having something similar to chiefdoms which had both limited power and cultural development. But by the 1300s, the Olmecs in their San Lorenzo settlement came to entirely new heights of cultural complexity. Looking at how sophisticated their art became, how majestic their huge statues were, and how big the city grew, archeologists concluded that San Lorenzo was unequaled by any other settlement in Mesoamerica at that time.

Besides being breathtakingly beautiful and intriguing for archeologists, these magnificent building projects of the Olmecs at San Lorenzo show that they had, at the very least, basic social and political stratification, with one small group of ruling elites and a large group of common people. Because without at least some social organization, such endeavors are practically impossible. Of course, since we don't have any written evidence, we can't be sure that they didn't manage to develop more finely diversified classes and to what extent their society was stratified. But looking at those impressive creations, it is evident that the Olmec rulers and elite were capable of mobilizing their population and force them to work in constructing architectural wonders. This meant Olmecan leaders held more power than their peers from other tribes around them. In fact, it could be argued that the power the ruling class held over their people is actually the most critical thing that differentiated Olmecs from other Mesoamerican people at the time.

The Olmec colossal head statue found at San Lorenzo.

That authority of the Olmec elite, which proved to be vital for their development as a civilization, was most likely based on the ruling classes controlling the fertile lands near the river, similarly to the elite in Ancient Egypt and Mesopotamia. And, unlike neighboring chiefdoms, the Olmec elite also managed to take control of trading with their neighbors. That allowed the Olmec ruling elite to become the elite, and gain command over the lower classes and force them to work on public projects, like building temples and statues. Of course, it should be kept in mind that this gathering of political authority and control of the Olmec elite didn't happen overnight, but was a slow process that lasted for a really long time.

Thanks to these factors, the Olmec settlement at San Lorenzo managed to keep its dominance for about three centuries, with its "Golden Age" lasting from about 1200 to 900 BCE. By the end of that era, it started to decline, losing its power and inhabitants. It became an empty shell of its previous glory. Historians aren't entirely sure what caused this downfall. Some think it could be due to natural problems like diseases or bad harvest years. Others believe it could be a result of an internal struggle for power or some kind of civil war. There were suggestions that an external military threat, either from neighboring Olmecs or some other tribes, managed to bring the San Lorenzo settlement to its knees. The one thing that archeologists are certain about is that by 800 BCE this city was pretty much abandoned. But that didn't mark the end of all Olmecs. As San Lorenzo started to fade, La Venta began to rise. And around 900 BCE it became the new center of power for the Olmecs and all of Mesoamerica.

Chapter 3 – Fading into Obscurity

As it usually happens in history, when one city or state falls, another rises to take its place. In the case of the Olmecs, La Venta took the place of San Lorenzo as the most important Olmec city during the 10th century BCE. As noted in the previous chapter, it likely wasn't a sudden change, but gradually happened. And under La Venta supremacy, Olmec civilization reached its peak. But unlike San Lorenzo, the natural swampy surroundings of La Venta wasn't quite suitable for farming, which raises the question of what gave that settlement the edge it needed to become the new center of Olmec power. Again, here is where historians disagree. One theory suggests that the Tonalá River had a different path at the time, so the swamps weren't as pervasive in that area. The other theory is that the La Venta Olmecs used nearby fertile lands as a source of food and labor by some way of occupation and exploitation. But considering that archeological surveys showed that the area of La Venta was settled as far back as 1750 BCE, the first option seems more likely, as it is more analogous to the San Lorenzo settlement.

Because of that, it's not unsurprising that La Venta based its own supremacy on a similar basis as San Lorenzo where the Olmec elite had the control of agricultural production and trading. But there was also one more crucial difference. Looking at the archeological evidence, historians concluded that this settlement also served as a religious and ceremonial center. This meant that the rulers of La Venta had even more power than their predecessors which probably spanned over a greater area, since this meant that all surrounding Olmecs came to La Venta, bringing offerings to their gods as well as the rulers of the city. With even more monumental buildings and statues that displayed their wealth and power than San Lorenzo, it is clear that the La Venta settlement reached greater heights than any city in Mesoamerica at the time, and it seems it had a lot to do with the religious aspect of the settlement.

But one should dismiss this site as a purely religious city. There is archeological evidence that it was a thriving town, with people living both in it and in the smaller settlements around it. And within that large number of residents, there were more specialists than in the older Olmec societies. Besides the priests and artisans that created the marvelous pieces of art the Olmecs are best known for today, there were traders, builders, and even indications of military-oriented professionals. We can only guess how many more professions and skilled laborers there were in La Venta. It is important to note that the Olmecs most likely weren't limited to just the ruling elite and working commoners at this time. Their society probably became more diverse based on their classes. With social complexity, Olmec culture also became more sophisticated.

Statue of an Olmec chief at La Venta.

Thanks to that complexity and sophistication of the Olmec society, for about five centuries, La Venta managed to maintain its dominance in both the Olmec civilization and the entire Mesoamerican region. But its power eventually started to decline. By 400 BCE, the La Venta settlement began to fade into obscurity. In the next century, the city was pretty much abandoned. Unlike San Lorenzo, archeologists are sure that the downfall of La Venta was a violent one, as they have found traces of a deliberate destruction of monuments and buildings. Although they aren't quite sure if the attack came from outside forces or if it was some kind of uprising, most believe it was a foreign power that invaded La Venta, since it is highly unlikely that the domestic population destroyed their own monuments. And although the Olmecs abandoned La Venta, the city didn't seem to lose its significance as a cultural center. Archeologists found buried offerings that are dated to the early Colonial Era that contain products like Spanish olives. This means that for more than a millennia people came back to this site to practice their religious rituals even though they forgot who built it and for what exact purpose. This is perhaps the best proof of how important and powerful the Olmecs and La Venta were.

However, this does not change the fact that at some point this settlement was abandoned. Whatever may be the exact cause, with the fall of this Olmec center, Olmec civilization also came to an end. And just like how we don't know exactly where they came from, we're not sure where they went, or to be more precise what happened to them. It is likely that most simply relocated or were assimilated into other cultures or some mixture of both. And assimilation with different cultures, which were so influenced by the Olmec civilization by this time, wasn't too much of a transition for most of the people. Ultimately, we can only be sure they didn't magically vanish or were all killed, as there is still some native population in the Olmec heartland that speaks a language that is descended from one we assume the Olmecs spoke.

Chapter 4 – Olmec Art

The first thing archeologists discovered about the Olmecs was their art, so it seems to be a fitting place to begin our journey to better understand their civilization. There wasn't some groundbreaking discovery of Olmecan sculptures or other art forms that brought them to light. For a long time, a lot of smaller statues and carvings from the Olmecs were circulating around the archeological artifact and ancient art markets. But most experts thought they were part of either Mayan or Aztec civilization or at least some derivation of those. So, they didn't attract much attention on their own. However, all of that changed in the second half of the 19th century when José Melgar y Serrano, one of the Mexican explorers, found the now famous Olmec colossal heads. After that discovery, the Olmecs were finally recognized as a separate and unique culture. At first many thought this strange new civilization flourished in about the same period as the Mayans and that they took over some aspects of Mayan culture which would explain the similarities between them. But opposed to them stood Matthew Sterling, archeologist of the Smithsonian Institute, who argued that the Olmecs predated others, such as the Mayans and Aztecs. The struggle between the two historical schools of Mesoamerican history was finally settled in the 1940s when Mexican archeologist Alfonso Caso managed to sway most of the scientific community to Sterling's side. Further carbon-dating tests, to the dismay of many Mayanists, people who were specialized in Mayan history, gave more conclusive support to the theory of Olmecs being one of the earliest known Mesoamerican civilizations.

The colossal heads that brought the Olmecs back into the limelight of history rightfully became the best-known symbol of their civilization and their art. Although all of them are rather big, they vary in sizes, weighing between 6 and 50 tons and ranging in height from 1.6 to 3.5 meters (5.2 to 11.4 ft). All of them were made from basalt mined in the Sierra de los Tuxtlas Mountains of Veracruz on the northern edge of what is now considered the Olmec heartland. These statues depict mature men with flat-faced and thick-lipped features, fleshy cheeks, and wearing various types of headgear that resemble today's rugby helmets. Because of those helmets, some researchers at first thought they represented winners and champions of some Mesoamerican ballgame, but that theory is now largely abandoned. They most likely represent rulers, considering they were the ones who had enough power to make that type of monument which researchers think took at least 50 years to carve out and move. Besides, the headgear is now usually associated with military or ceremonial symbolism.

One of the most prominent characteristics of these huge heads is naturalism, which is one of the staples of Olmec art in general. Naturalism means the art usually depicted real objects with natural, although typically stylized, features. The men depicted on those statues don't seem to be represented in an idealized image, but rather as the artists saw them. Some of them have a more serious look while others look like they are relaxed or even smiling. Since some traces of paint were found on them, there is a real possibility that they were brightly colored at the time of their construction. Of course, as time passed, the characteristics of the art style started to change a bit as well. So even though they are quite similar in style, there are slight differences between the earlier heads from San Lorenzo and the later ones from La Venta. The San Lorenzo ones seem to be more skillfully executed and more clearly realistic, while the La Venta ones show more of a tendency towards a more stylized art form.

While on the subject of the Olmec colossal heads, there is a myth about them that has to be debunked. Some researchers, after looking at the fat lips and other features of these monuments, claimed that they looked more like Africans than Mesoamericans and came to the conclusion that the Olmecs were of African origins. But various historians have since proven this wrong. By comparing these statues with the present-day native population living in the area, they showed that the features of the Colossal heads' faces were and still are common among Mesoamerican Indians. Also, other types of Olmec art don't depict those features as clearly or as much. Archeologists explain this fact by stating that basalt is different to work with compared to other materials that the Olmecs used. It is a harder substance that only allows shallow carvings on it, forcing the artists to make certain features on the faces that may not have been common among the Olmec population. With that being said, most of the scientific community disagree with this theory of Olmec African descent, putting it in more of a pseudohistory category.

Looking past the iconic colossal heads, the Olmecs also created other examples of monumental arts, such as altars and stelae. Made out of stone, they were decorated with beautiful carvings which showed off the Olmecs skill in both high and low reliefs. The most common depiction on these monuments was of an older person holding a child in his lap. Here it is seen that the Olmecs differ from most of the other cultures around the world since this iconography is usually connected with a mother-child motif. But in the Olmec reliefs, the older person is always shown as having masculine traits, which makes deciphering the meaning of these carvings rather tricky. Some scholars think they represent a connection with religion, displaying representations of deities. Others lean towards more of a dynastical meaning, like the passing of power from father to son. Of course, there were other motifs carved as well, like a clearer representation of rulers and priests, as well as warriors and animals, like snakes and jaguars. Almost all of them are created with the naturalistic style that was so common in the Olmec art. But the most stunning feature of their art is the capability of the Olmec artist to capture movement in their reliefs. Carving various scenes in which the subjects are caught in middle of an action, made their art feel more energetic.

Olmecs, of course, didn't only produce monumental art pieces. They are also quite well known for statues, small figurines, celts (ax-like tools), and pendants, all made from various materials with the most beautiful and finely-detailed ones made out of jade and serpentine. Since these were rare and precious stones, it is clear that those statues were made for the richest people in Olmec society, probably the royal family. They also made effigies and small ritual axes which held more of a ceremonial than practical purpose since they were never sharpened enough to be used. All of these art forms kept the distinctive Olmec style and were rooted in naturalism and realism. This style wasn't only bound to Olmec sculptures of various sizes, but was also represented in bowls and vessels made out of clay. They had intricate reliefs that showed stylized representations of animals and plants. In some cases, the bowls were even zoomorphic, shaped like animals.

One step further away from naturalistic characteristics and more towards the stylized type of Olmec art is the small baby-faced figurines. The name is quite self-explanatory, as the main features of these small statues are plump bodies, infantile puffy cheeks, swollen crying eyes, and pouty frowns. These babies are usually posed in a sitting or lying position, mimicking how little kids crawl and play on the ground. And although they are always depicted naked, there are no signs of gender on them. Another interesting characteristic of these figurines is that most of them have helmets on their heads, similar, if not identical, to those that crowned the Colossal heads. With that in mind, there is a possibility that the baby-faced sculptures are a representation of rulers' children, but their true purpose and iconographical meaning is yet to be determined.

But the most prominent exception to the typical naturalism of Olmec art are the motifs of were-jaguars, in which human form is mixed with the characteristics of a jaguar. And those motifs were surprisingly quite common for something that we mark as an exception. These are usually seen on sculptures, where ware-jaguars are often represented as infantile. They have chubby bodies and puffy-faced features, but also snarling mouths, toothless gums, or long fangs. In some cases, they also have claws. And like the previously mentioned baby-faced figurines, they were also sexless. One of the most common compositions that included were-jaguar babies is that of a larger adult figure holding the infant on outstretched arms like it's being presented. Looking at some of the finer details, like their usually cleft heads and decorations on their clothes, archeologists saw similarities with how later Mesoamerican civilizations represented their gods, which led them to believe that were-jaguars are a representation of a certain divine being, probably a rain deity. But like all other Mesoamerican cultures, the Olmecs also believed in a number of gods, so the question remains why the were-jaguars were so frequent and representations of other gods were not.

A classical were-jaguar sculpture from San Lorenzo.

Another interesting type of artifact made in the distinctive Olmec style are jade face masks. They have asymmetrical open, downturned mouths, wide nostrils, and half-squinting eyes, which suggests they are part of the Olmec tradition. However, archeologists have never found this kind of mask on any Olmec site to this day, even though most of them were created during the Olmec era. This has led some researchers to hypothesize that those masks were not made by Olmecs and were only influenced by their style. Others point out that wooden masks, made at the very beginning of the Olmec civilization, clearly show they had a long tradition of making masks. And they think it's only a matter of time until archeologists will find the jade masks at an Olmec site. Another interesting detail surrounding these masks is that one of them was recently found in an Aztecan tomb, even though carbon dating puts its creation date at around 500 BCE. This suggests that these masks were highly regarded throughout Mesoamerican history and it is highly possible that they were raided from Olmec sites by their successors.

Of course, the Olmecs made a lot of other artifacts and artwork. These were just some examples of the most well-known and noteworthy representations of their style. Although most of the Olmec art we talked about in this chapter was made from some kind of stone, precious minerals, or clay, Olmecs also used materials like cloth and wood to make their art. But since those other materials were less durable, almost no traces of those type of artifacts are left. And even though there are many questions and controversies surrounding Olmec art, like with their whole history, there is no denying its beauty, craftsmanship, and their influence on other Mesoamerican cultures that came after the Olmecs. Another testimony to the excellence of Olmec art is that centuries after they were gone, other civilizations saw their artifacts as priceless works of art. That is why those were praised and gathered, probably even traded by later civilizations. Also, some of the Olmec features and motifs were copied by artisans of other civilizations for thousands of years and have by now become the trademark of how we imagine Mesoamerican art. The influence of Olmec art on Mesoamerican society can be paralleled with the influence of ancient Roman and Greek art had on later European society.

Chapter 5 – The Olmec Traders

Even though the archeologists have given more attention to their art, trade was a much more important part of Olmec life and society and played a crucial role in their rise to power. It is significant to note that even though the Olmecs were the first to achieve a level of development that we associate with civilized life, they certainly weren't the only complex society in Mesoamerica, especially in the later periods of the Olmec era. Around them were many chiefdoms, which varied in cultural and social development as well as in wealth and power. And together with the Olmecs, they created a trade network which allowed not only transportation of materials and resources but also an exchange of ideas and culture. But the question arises of how the Olmecs differed from their neighbors; what allowed them to use trade for amassing riches better than others? How were they able to gather strength and influence through trading, and use it to develop their culture and flourish as a civilization?

Indeed, being situated in a vital trading hub that connected resource-rich areas of the present-day Yucatán peninsula and Central Mexico was undoubtedly helpful. But historians also think it was because the Olmecs were probably among the first to use long-distance trade rather than trading only with their nearest surrounding. With such a widespread trading network in place, the Olmecs were able to trade for the same types of resources with different tribes, while at the same time exporting their goods to numerous buyers. That diversity of trading partners is most likely what made their success in this field greater and easier, making their civilization richer than any other at the time. But archeologists think that the Olmecs didn't start trading to get wealthy. They believe it all started because their fertile and food-rich region lacked obsidian, a glass-like volcanic rock which was an essential resource for making farming and other work tools, weapons, decorative objects, and many other things. And even in the later stages of Olmec development, it seems that the core of their trade remained the basic need for that precious stone.

But obsidian wasn't the only resource that the Olmecs had to import. As the power and riches of their elite grew, so did their demand for materials needed for luxury items. That is why in later periods they started importing iron ore, serpentine, magnetite, and most importantly jade - which the Olmecs accessed by trading with Mayan predecessors in the Yucatán Peninsula and present-day Guatemala. Jade probably became the most widely used precious mineral in the Olmec society and was most commonly used to create masks and figurines. Using that as a connection, some historians who lean towards speculations and wild theories devised another theory about the origin of the Olmecs, connecting them with ancient China, specifically the Shang dynasty (1600-1000 BCE). According to that theory, Chinese refugees crossed the Pacific Ocean to form, or at least influence, the creation of the Olmec civilization. The major connections between the two civilizations was their usage and high regard of jade and the similarities between Olmec artwork and Chinese art that circulated in that period. Of course, these speculations are rejected by the majority of the Mesoamerican historians and archeologists as a wild tale.

Stepping away from the luxuries, it is interesting that there haven't been any traces of food being imported on a large scale by the Olmecs since their lands were fertile enough to sustain the population on their own. However, the Olmecs did trade for salt and cocoa. Although they had access to salt from the Gulf Coast, it seems it wasn't enough to satisfy their needs, considering they expanded their salt trade network in many directions—to the south towards present-day Guatemala, to the west to the Pacific Coast of Oaxaca, and to the north to the central plane of Mexico, which was later inhabited by the Aztecs. There is also a possibility that the Olmec traders weren't just bringing salt to use in their homeland, but were also reselling it to other tribes, acting as a middleman in the salt trade. That way salt became not only an important commodity needed to sustain life, but also a valued strategic resource needed for trading. Cocoa, on the other hand, was more of a luxury item which came to the Olmecs from the south, from what is today Honduras. There will be a more detailed explanation of the use and importance of cocoa in Olmec society in one of the following chapters.

Other goods they traded for were also animal pelts and feathers of exotic animals. The Olmec elite used these for both ceremonial purposes and as a sign of their status. In fact, when we combine all of the listed items the Olmec traders acquired, we can see that most of their import was focused on the need of the higher class. This could to a certain extent be explained by the fact that lower class could find most of the things they needed to survive in the Olmec heartland. And it also explains why the trade was mostly beneficial to the elite, while commoners saw little direct gain from it. Of course, we should keep in mind that the extra wealth that was brought into the Olmec society also benefited the whole population in the long run as it was one of the main driving forces of the development of their civilization. So it could be said that the non-elite parts of the society had at least some kind of indirect benefit from the development of trade, even though the goods imported to their lands were not meant for their use.

So far, we have seen what goods the Olmecs brought into their country. But they also had a lot to offer in return. As we already know, the Olmec region was quite fertile, boasting various types of food like squash, beans, manioc, sweet potato, and most importantly maize. Not only that, but they lived next to the ocean and big rivers where they had access to fish, another important food group. So, it is reasonable to assume that food was one of the first resources they offered to their trade partners as it was their first step towards establishing their trade network they are now famous for — in the earliest stages of their civilization and their trade. Clearly food was the foundation of the Olmec trade. It should be mentioned that in the early Olmec era the extent of their trade was still limited to the local vicinity, trading only with their immediate neighbors. It took a while for the Olmecs to develop this significant part of their economy, which allowed them to move up from basic food trade.

Even though food most likely remained an essential part of their trade even in the later periods, as the Olmec civilization developed so did the skills of their various artisans. And since they seemed to be the first ones to achieve a certain level of intricacy and finesse, they also realized that others might be interested in products their craftsmen had to offer. So, in later periods, the Olmec traders started exporting their artisanal and artistic creations. These varied from ritual figurines and masks, to various pottery which held both aesthetic and practical use, to clothing and everyday life tools. As the artisanal craftworks were not as common, especially during the San Lorenzo supremacy, they were more valuable, giving Olmec traders the upper hand in trading with others. Creating these goods from the raw materials they imported and exporting them for higher prices allowed the Olmecs to amass wealth quickly. In fact, we could draw a parallel between the ancient Olmecs and Industrial Age Britain. Both of those powers used their technical advances and knowhow to transform imported raw materials in finished products they would then trade for much higher prices, making a considerable profit. But the Olmecs also had something else to export besides the handcrafts and food.

Although the Olmecs lacked many natural resources other than food, their region was rich with trees used to produce primitive rubber. The Olmecs were, unsurprisingly, the first to start harvesting the natural sap of the Hevea tree to make the rubberlike material. It's not surprising that the Olmecan traders used it as an important part of their exports due both to the scarcity of the product and the numerous applications it could be used for. We can assume rubber was a valuable product at the time, and it is certain that it played an important role in prestige and prosperity of the Olmec traders. That prestige was also important for them to make the next step in utilizing their trade network – assuming the role of middleman traders. They were able to assume this role partly because of their geographical location, but also because they were seen as reliable traders thanks to their reputation. And this type of trade is probably the most profitable, as it requires no effort in creating a product, and it brings pure gain. Of course, the role of a trade intermediary wasn't something the Olmec traders could do from the beginning. Only after they established their extensive trade network, connections and reputation were they able to fulfill this very profitable part of the trade.

But there is one last piece of the puzzle left that gives one more reason why the Olmecs were such successful traders, and which gave them the edge over their competitors. That was the monopoly in trade. It is true that the initial spark that lit the raging fire of the Olmecan trade was their geographical position, which allowed them to trade with almost all of Mesoamerica. But more importantly, they had a monopoly over the items they traded. They had the best artisans whose skillfully crafted products were unmatched for a long time and the unique rubber that was distinctive to their region. It is true, however, that the Olmecs lacked obsidian, jade, salt, and other resources which should have put them on equal footing to other chiefdoms and tribes. But that wasn't the case because many different tribes had the same resources the Olmecs needed. That meant they could choose different trading partners according to their needs and current circumstances. On the other hand, those tribes had no other choice than to trade with them for the unique items the Olmecs had to offer. That is the crucial last component in the success of the Olmec traders.

Chapter 6 – The Olmecs and Their Neighbors

It should be clear by now that the Olmecs weren't alone in the jungles and plains of Mesoamerica. Even in the earliest parts of their civilization's formation and development, they were surrounded by many other settlements, tribes, and people. The Olmecs not only prospered thanks to their trade with these neighbors but also gathered the power that came with the wealth they amassed and influence which came from their prestige. Those factors became instrumental to the rise of their society from obscurity into the civilized world. But it would be unwise to think that trade, no matter how important it was to them, were the only relations they had with surrounding tribes. However, it is still unclear to this day what the exact nature of these interactions and connections was. Without any clear evidence, there is plenty of room for uncertain theories. But, like before, that fact shouldn't stop us in search of the Olmec story.

Archeologists started to question the relationships the Olmecs held with other tribes from the early days of their exploration of the Olmec civilization and history. Going from the fact that many Olmec-styled artifacts were found over a wide area of Mesoamerica, those early researchers of the Olmecs came to the natural conclusion that at least at some point there was a clear supremacy of that civilization over the whole region. Archeologists theorized that the number of their artifacts found in settlements far from the Olmec heartland meant they directly controlled those settlements. That led them to think that the Olmecs had sort of an empire, similar to the one the Romans had in the Mediterranean. But during the mid-20th century with further archeological digs and findings, this theory became less attractive to historians as evidence that corroborated this theory was almost nonexistent. With the lack of proof of any kind, it became clear that the Olmecs didn't manage to unify Mesoamerica into one large empire.

Yet, historians were unable to leave this idea completely. In their minds, signs of Olmec supremacy were still there since all their artifacts were scattered around the region. So, some of them thought that if the Olmecs didn't subdue Mesoamerica with their direct control, they must have made colonies out of their neighbors. Either the local elites stayed in power, paying their respect and tributes to their Olmec masters, similar to the medieval vassals. Or they were removed and substituted by the Olmec officials as the Europeans did with their colonies in the 19th century. This more indirect rule could also explain the wide area of their supremacy, as in both types of colonist rule the locals would have tried to replicate Olmec art and would have close trading ties with the Olmecs themselves. That would explain all the artifacts found. But as with the previous theory of a large Mesoamerican empire, this was also more or less rejected by the majority of historians in recent years. The reason is the same – there is no clear foundation for it in the archeological findings. The most widely supported idea currently is that Olmec supremacy was rooted in their culture and trade alone, without any forcible subjugation of their neighbors.

The explanation of all the archeological findings of Olmec and Olmec styled artifacts scattered around Mesoamerica, in non-Olmecan settlements, became less based on violence and force. For once, historians finally accepted the possibility that the Olmec trade network was so vast and well-connected that their handcrafts could have reached much further than they thought before. Also, with the acknowledgment of their trading success as well as the recognition of their artisanal quality, historians now believe that their products would have been sought among their neighbors as a sign of prestige, as luxury items. And the explanation for the artifacts that weren't Olmec made, but only Olmec styled can be quite simple. Local artisans tried to copy their work as Olmec art, and since crafts were a sign of high status, even "knockoffs" could be valuable, as not everyone could afford the original Olmec creation. Now there are even some theories that the Olmecs were in a way exporting their artisans as well, meaning that rulers and elites of other chiefdoms who had enough wealth and power could hire Olmec artisans to create art for them. By now it has become more apparent that the Olmec rule was more localized to the Olmec heartland.

But knowing that the Olmecs were only ruling over their own region is only a partial answer to the question relating to the nature of the relationship they had with their neighbors. From new evidence found at both Olmec and non-Olmec sites across Mesoamerica, historians now think that relations between the chiefdoms and tribes were more on the equal footing and interlinked than it was thought before. This was definitely true in the later era of the Olmec civilization when the surrounding cultures managed to catch up with them in their level of development. That allowed for more complicated diplomatic relations between the Olmecs and their neighbors. One example of this rise in sophistication of tribal diplomacy is found at the archeological site of Chalcatzingo in the Valley of Morelos, located in the southern portion of the Central Highlands of present-day Mexico. That location was settled by an unnamed tribe as early as 1500 BCE, but it remained at a rather low level of development until 900 BCE when they came in contact with the Olmecs and started to emulate their style. They reached the height of their power between 700 and 500 BCE, at the time of La Venta supremacy. With the high number of Olmec products found at Chalcatzingo, archeologists have concluded they had a close relationship between each other and also believed there was an alliance between them that was most likely strengthened with a marriage.

The connections and diplomacy between the Olmecs and their neighbors were also likely fostered by personal visits and connections between rulers and members of the elite. These actions certainly helped the Olmecs to forge good relations with surrounding tribes. This shouldn't come as a big surprise considering that the trade was controlled by the upper classes of most cultures and civilizations in the early era of Mesoamerican history. From that we can clearly see that the backbone of the diplomatic relations was indeed trade. And profit seems to be the most likely reason why all of the elites strived for rather peaceful and good neighboring policies, as war meant that the trade would stop and that would be bad for all sides involved. One could even claim that rulers of these chiefdoms, including the Olmecs, were thinking more like merchants than generals. Of course, even though the Olmecs seem to be an overall peace-loving society of traders doesn't necessarily mean they didn't resort to violence and aggression towards some smaller villages around them to impose a diplomatic or trade agreement upon them or offer them protection from other chiefdoms or even from the Olmecs themselves. After all, if there was no outside threat, why would any tribe or state create alliances with their neighbors? Also, some historians also speculate that the Olmecs used their military power and diplomatic influence to interfere in local politics of some smaller tribes and settlements. That way they could favor the local elite who would benefit them and their trade more. This one more testament to the complicated nature of the Olmec diplomacy, and their relations with other Mesoamerican tribes.

It should be emphasized that all of the possibilities mentioned in this chapter are at the present time speculations and theories based on scant evidence, so the true nature of Olmec intertribal relations and diplomacy remain shrouded in the veil of mystery. At least until some new evidence sheds more light on this. And even though some theories are more likely than others, the historic community isn't able to completely agree on them. Thus, this question of how exactly the Olmecs interact with their neighbors remains open for the time being, but nevertheless, it is an essential piece of the puzzle in the Olmec story.

Chapter 7 – Olmec Military

In the previous chapter, it was shown that the Olmecs weren't an expansionistic and bloodthirsty society, but rather wealth-searching and peace-loving traders who avoided going to war. But that shouldn't lead to the conclusion that they didn't have any soldiers or weapons. Even in non-violent civilizations, there had to be some sort of a military to protect them from foreign threats and invaders, especially if they were as rich as the Olmecs were. Some historians tried to link the lack of defensive fortifications and walls around the Olmec settlements as a sign that they weren't threatened in their heartland and from that drew conclusions that the Olmec army didn't actually exist. But after more research, archeologists found evidence that confirms that the Olmecs had some sort of military, though the exact details about it are still debated about.

Like in most of the ancient civilizations worldwide, the military in the Olmec society was linked to the elite and the ruling class. This is most obvious in their art, as rulers were often depicted wearing helmets and carrying various types of weapons. Opponents against the idea of the Olmec military's existence tried to explain this art by suggesting that those weapons and armor had a more ceremonial and religious purpose, rather than practical. And it is likely that military equipment had some ritual importance and was a sign of power and prestige. But other evidence suggests that the equipment was used for more than just its symbolism. For one, in some artistic depictions, Olmec rulers are accompanied by naked and bound men.

These were most likely captives from some sort of military endeavor, as the burned bones were found in some burial pits. It has been suggested that those were remains of foreigners, since the Olmecs buried their dead. It is also probable that they believed, like most other Mesoamerican civilizations, that burning the body would damn the soul of the deceased. So, for some historians, the logical explanation of why a large group of adult males would be desecrated like this would be if they were prisoners of war, captured during a battle by the ruling elite.

These artistic portrayals clearly show that the Olmecs had an actual army and that it was in the hands of the higher class. However, lack of written evidence limits our insight into the details of how exactly their military worked. That is why maybe the best source for a deeper understanding of this topic comes from the Olmec weapons which were found at archeological sites. In the early San Lorenzo period, the most commonly used weapons were fire-hardened wooden spears, which were both primitive and inefficient. So, it is likely they were used primarily for hunting rather than for war. But as that settlement started its golden age and trade expansion around 1150 BCE, the Olmecs also adopted an important innovation in their military equipment. They started using obsidian tips for their spears, which made them sharper, with longer edges that could also be used for both slashing and stabbing. Judging by some sculptures of that period, Olmecs also adopted the use of clubs and maces, which are more primitive type of shock weapons. This is an important step, since for the first time, weapons were made with a solely martial application and were not mere adaptations of everyday utilitarian tools. And as with many other things, it could be argued that the Olmecs were the first to make that kind of leap, giving them an edge in the arms race of ancient Mesoamerica.

An Olmec king holding a mace-like weapon.

Beside those hand-to-hand weapons, there is evidence that the Olmecs also used throwing spears and atlatls, which is a spear-throwing tool common in the Mesoamerican region. But their use seems to be limited since they would be ineffective in fights against raiders and in smaller skirmishes, which were probably the most common type of battles the Olmecs faced. Besides, the supply of projectiles would quickly be exhausted rendering them quite useless, especially in conflicts that are further away from their heartland. But probably more interesting is the fact that the Olmecs didn't use any kind of armor. Their soldiers are usually depicted without any protective gear on their bodies, with the exception of helmets. And archeologists think that those helmets were probably more a symbol of status rather than functional protection for the head. Not only that, but the Olmec warriors were never depicted carrying a shield. Some historians believe the reason behind this is that they needed extra mobility in hand-to-hand combat, while others think they didn't have advanced enough technology yet to build armor which offered enough protection while at the same time not weigh too much. Some even argue that armor in general wouldn't be useful against opponents who used hit-and-run tactics, which were probably the most common type of adversaries the Olmecs met. The use of armor spread through Mesoamerica only when most armies became more conventional in nature, but by that time the Olmecs had already faded into obscurity.

But the Olmec had one more crucial military contribution to give before they disappeared. That was another new weapon, a slingshot, which appeared among the Olmecs during the La Venta dominance. Archeologists aren't sure if they originally created it or if they adopted it from some other tribe, but from the archeological evidence that is scattered across Mesoamerica, historians believe that the slingshot was spread throughout the region by the Olmecs. It was at the time the most superior long-range weapon of the region. Unlike throwing spears, its ammunition was less likely to run out, as small stone projectiles could be carried in larger quantities. And they could be replenished pretty much everywhere, even on an expedition long away from home. Slingshots also had a much higher rate of fire than throwing spears. The biggest advantage of a slingshot, however, was their range, which in a best-case scenario was up to 500 meters (about 550 yards). When we take into account that the Mesoamerican soldiers weren't equipped with any kind of armor, a hit from a single slingshot projectile could be quite damaging, if not deadly if it landed in the right spot. This new weapon gave an edge to the Olmec forces in both offensive and defensive actions, and historians think it was also rather useful against the hit-and-run raids on merchant caravans.

The implementation of the slingshot surely changed the military strategy that the Olmecs used. But we can only give educated guesses to the exact tactic that might have been used by the Olmec warriors because there's no evidence about it at all - not even on statues and carvings. The main question is if they used any kind of cohesive formation. From other examples around the world, it is known that armies which used shock weapons like the Olmecs did often had at least some kind of simple formation that allowed the soldier to focus on the enemy in front of him while his fellow warriors protected his sides and back. It is possible that the Olmecs used some simple tactical formation which would allow this, but most military historians think that it's not likely. For one, their opponents didn't have organized armies and most likely used guerilla strategies, so the Olmecs wouldn't be able to utilize the advantages of the tactical formation. Also, the fact that they already had technical superiority meant that the Olmecs didn't have to bother with learning new ways of warfare. Also, formations require at least some kind of military training. And there is no compelling evidence for that. Thus, it is far more likely that the battles were fought more on an individual scale. They would start as a mass confrontation between two armies, but due to the lack of organized tactics, the fight would break into duels between two soldiers. But with the implementation of slingshots, it is possible that a primitive type of tactic was developed, where first the projectiles were fired in volleys and then the hand-to-hand combat commenced.

Apart from the tactics used, the size of the Olmec army is also an important and interesting issue. As the total Olmec population wasn't really that high, reaching in the most optimistic estimates about three hundred thousand in the heartland, their armies wouldn't be that large. The second limiting factor was the handling of new types of weapons. It required some specialized training for a soldier to be proficient with it, and common folks couldn't just derive military skills from their utilitarian usage of tools. This means that war became the business of the elite, who could afford the time to gain military expertise. Common people played only a secondary role in the army. With that in mind, the largest possible army the Olmecs could create, at least in theory, was around five thousand strong. And that is if we consider the whole Olmec heartland as the source for raising the army, which was also highly unlikely as there is no evidence that the Olmecs were united into a single state. In reality, their armies were a lot smaller than that. One more reason for the limited number of the Olmec troops was the necessity of developed logistics needed to sustain an army of a larger size for a more extended period or on a long-distance campaign. That was one area in which no matter how advanced the Olmec society was, it wasn't efficient enough.

Taking all these facts into consideration leads us to a conclusion that the true nature of the Olmec military was mostly linked with armed trading caravans. For one, both merchants and warriors came from the elite class and likely performed both tasks at the same time. Secondly, these were rather small parties whose primary goal was to protect the goods. Thirdly, their equipment and tactics weren't designed for large-scale battles, but more for small skirmishes with bandits and raiders. Ultimately, the role of the Olmec military was protective, not expansionistic. But it remained powerful enough to influence their trading partners and neighbors with the idea of their strength and capabilities. With that influence, the Olmecs were able to expand and maintain their trading network, making local elites of other tribes more willing to cooperate with them, providing more secure trading than before. In the end, even the military revolved and evolved around trading, which seems to be the backbone of the whole Olmec civilization.

Chapter 8 – The Olmecs at Home

So far, we have focused more on how the Olmecs interacted with their neighbors and surrounding tribes. But now it's time to ask the question of how the Olmecs' life and society were structured. These questions are important in understanding the Olmecs and their story. Especially considering that the story of the common people is often unintentionally neglected in ancient history because they weren't the moving force behind substantial historical events which meant that they left less of a trail of evidence after them. This is why in this chapter, we shall try to uncover as many details about the Olmec commoners as the archeological findings allow us.

The first significant question about the common Olmecs is what they did for a living since we know that the elite was busy with trade and military. It shouldn't be a big surprise that, like most of the other commoners in the ancient world, the lower classes of the Olmec society were mainly farmers working on fields which were located outside of their villages. As we mentioned before, they grew maize, squash, beans, sweet potato, and manioc. Besides farmers, there were fishermen, either on the rivers or on the Golf Coast, who brought in fish, crabs, turtles, snakes, and shellfish. As the Mesoamericans didn't develop herding until the Europeans came, they still had hunters providing meat to supplement the vegetable and fruit diet. They caught rabbits, possums, raccoons, peccary (also known as skunk pig), and even deer. Also, they hunted for birds as well. It should be mentioned that those animals weren't used only for meat, but also for their hide and feathers which were used in various products and handicrafts made by artisans. These professions were the foundation of the Olmec society on which all others were built upon. But they were the least influential strata in it and were in a way exploited and controlled by the elite class which took the fruits of their labor for themselves and at the same time made them work on their grand project.

The common people, in most cases, didn't live in the central towns like San Lorenzo or La Venta. Instead, they lived in the villages that surrounded them. Common villages were rather small, with scattered wooden shacks and in some cases, if the village was large enough, even a small temple. They usually searched for higher ground to build up their villages and surrounding them were the fields most of them worked on. Of course, their wooden homes were rather modest and small. But they usually had a nearby garden which was used to grow medicinal and cooking herbs they needed for everyday life. Also, most of them had at least one storage pit dug nearby, which they used to preserve food, similar to the function of a root cellar. But their lives gravitated towards the center of town to which their village was associated, as they were the true social, political, economic, and religious centers of the Olmec society where the elite lived. The true nature of the elite-commoners relationship is unknown to us. We can't be sure if the villagers or the higher class owned the land, nor if or how exactly the commoners paid tributes. And if they did pay, how did the elite justify taxes? Were they paying for the land use or for protection, be it from outside attacks or from the elites themselves? Was the subordination of the commoners rooted in religion? All these and much more are still unknown to us, and at this stage, the only thing we could do is merely guess.

Another distinctive class, in a broad meaning of the word, were artisans, from those that created the wonderful pieces of the Olmec art, to those who created tools and weapons, to builders, etc. They probably resided in both villages and towns centers, but certainly more in the latter. On a social scale, they were probably a step above the farmers since their work involved skilled labor. And more importantly, their products and craftsmanship were sought by the elite, making them a bit more valuable, especially considering they were less numerous than the farmers. While some of them could have gained access to a cozy way of life if they were really good in their craft, they were by no means near the elite. We can't even compare them to the middle class of our time. Artisans were definitely still a lower class, nowhere near the elite, who most likely lumped them together with the farmers. That is why the elite had no problem to exploit their products for their own gain, like they did with the farmers. Although, as we've seen from the idea of export of artisans, if an artisan would show a high enough level of skill, he could gain a considerable level of respect from the higher class, which was clearly not possible for the farmers.

Other details about the everyday life of the lower class Olmecs are pretty much unknown. The things we can say with a degree of certainty is that there were no schools, as there is not even a hint for it among the archeological findings. Not even in the elite circles. Any education they got came from their families and neighbors. The cultural and religious life was centered in towns, as well as the trade. So, the commoners from surrounding villages had to commute to the towns if they wanted to participate in those spheres of life. Also, by looking at the scale of buildings and monuments in the town centers, we can assume that the elite had a way of mobilizing those villagers to participate in those great public projects. Some historians think it was done by use of religion, while others associate it with the use of force. Another possibility is that, like in some other ancient civilizations around the world, public work labor was one of the ways to pay taxes. But not all is so gray for the Olmec commoners. As they lived in relative peace, they had calm although hardworking lives. When this is compared with some other examples in history, it wasn't all that bad.

Another part of the everyday life of the Olmecs — that is rather unimportant when compared with others we have talked about, yet quite interesting — are the clothes they wore. And unlike most of the other topics, thanks to the archeological evidence we can talk about this with more certainty. For men, the most common thing they wore was a simple loincloth, usually without any decoration on it. This isn't surprising considering the warm climate in which the Olmecs lived. In some cases though, they did wear tunics or mantles, most likely on some special occasions like ceremonies and religious rituals. Women also kept it rather simple, wearing only dresses and belts. As the evidence for this lays in the stone carvings and other forms of art, since no actual textile has been preserved, we can only give educated guesses on the exact material the Olmec clothes were made from. The most likely candidates are cotton and possibly in some cases leather. It also seems that these types of clothing were the same for both elite and commoners, with the difference being the quality of the textile and some minor decorations and color.

A carving of an Olmec woman.

Now, this doesn't mean that you wouldn't be able to differentiate a member of the elite from a commoner if you saw them next to the other. The biggest and most obvious distinction between these two classes would be the headdresses the elite wore. Unlike other types of clothing, these were complex and adorned with various decorations like beads, bird feathers, and tassels. The assumption is that the larger and more majestic examples shown in the Olmec art were reserved for ceremonies, while in everyday life they wore something that would be more similar to a simple turban. It is also rather interesting to note that there are representations of hats with brims, which are rather uncommon in the pre-Columbian Mesoamerica. The Olmec elite is also commonly seen in art having various adornments and jewelry on them. Those ranged from nose and ear plugs, through bracelets and anklets, to pendants and necklaces. These pieces of jewelry were usually made from jade and other precious stones, with the possibility that in some cases the less wealthy had them made from other perishable materials like wood.

Alas, it is time to turn our attention away from the fun and exciting story of fashion and trinkets, back to more serious topics. We have to examine the roles the Olmec elite played in everyday life. They were a clear minority in the Olmec society like elites usually are in all cultures around the world. They lived almost exclusively in the town centers, like Tres Zapotes or La Venta, where they enjoyed all the benefits of being the ruling class. Their homes were larger, built from more durable materials than wood, and decorated with various art pieces. And unlike the lower classes, they didn't have to work as hard, and it could be even hypothesized that they had servants of some sorts, though there is no clear indication of slavery. Taking into account that in the later Mesoamerican cultures slavery wasn't common nor had it played a substantial role, we can assume it also wasn't an important part of the Olmec society. Another perk of being a member of the elite was traveling. Thanks to trade, they were not only able to amass wealth, but also journey across the region, which wasn't something that the commoners did much. With more free time, members of the elite could focus more on religious ceremonies, feasts, and also on learning new important skills. Looking at all of that, their lives seemed to be quite carefree, with the only worry being how to better show off their power and riches and confirm their place at the top of the social hierarchy.

This is a good moment to repeat one more time that the rule of the elite over the commoners was rooted in their command over three things: religion, trade, and military. With the development of more sophisticated weapons, the military power of the elite grew substantially, because for one, only the elite knew how to use them proficiently. Also, those new types of weapons were something that a common farmer could not afford. As a result, the Olmec elite became distinctively stronger than the lower class. That made most of the rebellions of the commoners futile. And as the trade grew, it became harder for a commoner to get into the merchant circles, if not impossible. Also, wealth allowed the elite to amass more influence and power. For example, it made connecting with elites of other tribes possible, which amplified their political dominance. And as the rich had more time to practice their fighting skills, the elite also expanded its military domination.

The last segment, religion, is where things become a bit less clear. We cannot be sure how and when the elite grabbed this power. Some speculate that it began way before the Olmecs started developing their civilization. At the time, when the Olmecs' ancestors first switched to agriculture, a certain group of people or individuals may have gained a level of expertise in the calendar. With that skill, they could have helped with the harvesting of food, which would seem to others like they were talking to the gods through the skies. Or the first religious leaders came from the early military leaders who achieved victories which benefited the whole community and were seen as magical. Another possibility is that they gained their divine recognition when they were able to mobilize other common populations for building temples and shrines.

Whatever may be the root of it, it is certain that the Olmec elite had a dogmatic religious role in their society, which wasn't that uncommon. We can simply look at ancient Egypt as a comparison, where the pharaoh was a god on the earth. Some have theorized that the Olmec chiefs had the same divine justification for their rule, but this is uncertain. With these characteristics in mind, some historians have tried to label the rule of the Olmec elite as a form of military theocracy. With that came the debate if the Olmecs had developed a state or not. In this debate, there are two sides. One claims that the Olmec society wasn't diffused enough, with only two social classes, and that the rule of the elite wasn't sophisticated enough. With that, they meant that the elite didn't develop a mechanism of what we think as proper government. That part of the historian community is more willing to label the Olmec rule as a chiefdom, which is seen as a transitional type of rule that evolved from egalitarian tribes of the prehistoric times towards a fully developed state. The opposing side points to the major public projects as proof of the firm control the elite held over the masses. The sheer complexity of the Olmec culture is more than enough for historians to conclude that the Olmecs had a state. But no matter how historians label it, the rule of the elite was more or less absolute.

While on the subject of the Olmecs rule in their heartland, there is also an important question that has to be answered—were the Olmecs united in a single state/chiefdom? Some historians believe that they had to be in order to achieve such a success in both spreading their culture and trading. The lack of defensive fortifications and signs of serious battles in the Olmec heartland indicate that they lived in peace among each other (some form of military confrontation would also be expected if there was no political unity among them). But on the other side, there are no clear indications that the major town centers were in any way politically connected. The connection via culture is evident but looking at ancient Greece and the Mayans, one can see that sharing a culture does not necessarily mean a unified state. That is why some historians tend to believe the idea that the Olmecs were divided into several smaller city-states. Evidently close ties between those city-states could be identified as the alliance among the elites, possibly even with arranged marriages. And if those alliances were interconnected, there is also a chance that the Olmecs even had a sort of a league of city-states. Connection of that type would help them present a more unified front towards all of their neighbors, helping them with the trade. At the same time, the league would help to keep the peace between the city-states, explaining the lack of fortifications.

Chapter 9 – Religion and Beliefs of the Olmecs

As stated in previous chapters, religion played an essential role in the Olmec society. It was a source that legitimized the rule of the elites. And we have seen that the town centers were also used as ceremonial and religious centers. This status gave them enormous prestige and drew crowds from other settlements to come and pay their respects in both offering and prayer. But how was the Olmecs' religion structured? What did they believe in? Luckily for us, the Olmecs left us traces in their art, as well as in the religions of their successors, like the Mayans and the Aztec. Even though we don't have the exact knowledge of their rituals, we have a general idea of what they believed in.

It is generally accepted that the Olmec rulers played an important, if not central, part of religious practices. They may even have been seen as a representation of god(s) on earth. Beside them, there were also full-time priests, whose only concern was maintaining rituals, performing ceremonies, and appeasing the gods. They were almost certainly connected with the temples, like in other ancient civilizations. One of their jobs as priests was also to connect with the spiritual powers through various disciplines like meditating, fasting, and even ritualistic self-harming. Some scholars even go so far as to claim that the Olmecs also practiced human sacrifices, even though there is no hard evidence for that. It is possible that the ritual self-harming of the Olmecs was a stepping stone towards human sacrifice of the later Mesoamerican cultures. But it is evident that religion was mostly centralized and revolved around the temples in the major city centers.

There is one last possible religious figure in the Olmec society, and that is the shaman. They were likely remnants from the non-organized religion of their ancestors, linked more with the commoners. And unlike priests, it is likely that every village and community had one. Their exact practices are unknown, but after looking at other indigenous people of the Americas, scholars think that they were likely focused on altering the human state of mind with hallucinogens, trying to transcend human consciousness and connect with animals like the jaguar. That is why some archeologists think they wore masks that represented the were-jaguar, a mixture of human and jaguar, which as we already know was a common motif in the Olmec art. Some also link these shamans with astronomers and astrologists, or even possibly with the medicine-men. But it's clear that they were focused on helping their community in everyday life.

Based on available evidence, shamans were somewhat an opposite to the town priests. The priests were focused on the larger questions of religion, tasked with pleasing the gods, practicing ceremonies, and giving and taking the offerings. Their role was in the grander scheme of the universe. Shamans, on the other hand, weren't focused on praying to the gods as much as trying to understand and interpret their action. They were focused on smaller problems that on a large scale weren't as important to the whole Olmec society. But they played an important role in the local communities. We can assume that as the Olmec civilization grew stronger and more developed, the balance between shamans and priests shifted. In the beginning, they were equally important, at least to the common people. But in later periods, when priests got their large temples and gained more authority as well as a monopoly on the religious issues, significance and prestige of shamans dropped. It is something that is common for all early civilizations of the world during the process of moving towards what we today call organized religion.

Moving away from the subject of rituals and ceremony, it is time to see what and who the Olmecs believed in. We know that they were polytheists who believed in a number of gods, though we don't know their exact names. Their view of the universe was through energy and spiritualism linked closely with animals. That is evident from the fact that their gods were in shapes of different animals, sometimes even crossed with humans or with other animals. Their exact roles as gods are a matter of speculation, but they were certainly linked to various natural phenomena which were essential to preserving life such as the sun or rain. As previously mentioned, the were-jaguar was represented the most in Olmec art, which led many early archeologists to recognize it as the most important deity of the Olmecs. But recently, more scholars see it as one of the equals in the Olmec pantheon of the gods. The most widely accepted role of the were-jaguar is as the rain deity, but some also link it with military and/or sexual conquest. It is certain that the jaguar was an animal that played an important part in the lives of the Olmec. It was a fierce predator, hunting both day and night, which gave the feeling of raw power to it. It also seemed to represent the unification of three elements, water, air, and land. That symbolism comes from the fact that they lived in the jungle where they were comfortable walking on the ground, swimming in the rivers and climbing way up onto the trees. It is possible that the Olmecs wanted to emulate that energy and that is why they revered it so much.

Another important deity was the feathered or plumed serpent. This iconography may be recognizable to those who have heard about Quetzalcoatl of the Aztecs or Kukulkan of the Mayans. Many speculate that these two cultures adopted this deity from the Olmec tradition. From these later societies, we know they respected the plumed serpent as the creator of humanity as well as a hero who played a messianic role, promising to lead the humans to some kind of a better future. Interestingly, it was able to shift its roles between a god, human hero, and an intangible myth. Even its mixture of a snake and a bird represented its important dualism and ability to change. A bird represented more divine attributes. Because it can fly, it can be close to the sky. And flight was a representation of its godly virtues. But a snake represented more down to earth attributes, since they were less virtuous and more human. The reason for that kind of symbolism was the fact that the snake crawled on the ground and dirt, far away from the divinity of the sky. That dualism represented the idea of transformation and inconsistency in life. But at the same time, being constantly around it represented some more permanent aspects of life, that can't be so easily transformed. Even though we clearly see that they revered this god, its importance to the Olmec culture is uncertain. As in some later Mesoamerican civilizations, the plumed serpent deity was the most significant in the pantheon, which was even divinely linked with rulers, so some thought it was important to the Olmecs as well. That is why in earlier periods of the Olmec research, some archeologists believed that the Olmec rulers were identified with this god in particular. But now, not everyone is so convinced, as this deity isn't as prevalent in the Olmec art, and there are no signs of its prestige among other gods.

The oldest representation of feathered serpent in Mesoamerica found at La Venta.

There were numerous other gods as well within the Olmec pantheon. There was a maize deity which is commonly represented with a cleft on its head with corn sprouting from it. In some cases, it also had a jaguar snarl on it, again showing the mysterious connection the Olmecs had with this animal. Usually on par with the maize god is the water god, which looks like a baby were-jaguar. The water god was connected to all water, including lakes and rivers. They seem to be paired together because maize and water were the sources of survival for the Olmecs. They also revered an anthropomorphic shark or fish creature. It is recognizable by its crescent eyes and a shark tooth. Some think it was the god of the underworld. Another important deity was the so-called Olmec dragon, which is a crocodile-looking god, with an occasional addition of human, jaguar or eagle features. It seems to have represented the Earth and fertility. As such, it was connected to agriculture, fertility, and fire. Of course, there are more that scholars haven't identified or singled out yet, but these examples seem to be the most important.

But the level of their importance to the Olmec society isn't entirely certain yet. Some earlier scholars were even doubtful if these were true representations of the gods the Olmecs believed in, although that is the currently accepted theory. The connections of deities and their roles are in some cases guesses based on connections with later cultures and their religions. Even their mutual ties are uncertain. Still, the biggest mystery of the Olmec beliefs remains the issue of the were-jaguar and its importance to the Olmecs. But no matter what the truth is behind these supernatural beings that were such an important motif of the Olmec art and focus of reverence, one thing is certain: their religious beliefs formed a complex and structuralized system. And from the ability to compare them with similar deities from other later Mesoamerican civilization, as well as the fact that some of their shrines were worshiped by people long after they were gone, scholars concluded that the Olmec beliefs became the foundation of others in the region. Though this shouldn't come as much of a surprise, in ancient times, gods were shared among civilizations like any other idea.

Chapter 10 – Cultural Innovation of the Olmecs

It has been mentioned in many places how the Olmecs were able to influence their successors in numerous ways, creating a foundation of the Mesoamerican culture as a whole, from trade networks and theocratic rule to religion and art. That was a remarkable feat on its own. But they also seem to be responsible for quite a few important cultural innovations which in later periods became the very things most people identify with pre-Columbian Mesoamerica. And some of these are still unmistakably a part of the present-day Mesoamerican culture. These cultural innovations are probably the very things that justify the idea of the Olmecs being the mother culture to all others in the Mesoamerican region which is another testament to their power and influence.

Architecturally speaking, probably the most iconic buildings seen in Mesoamerican cultures are the pyramids. Only slightly less famous than the pyramids found in Egypt, these Mesoamerican creations have been in the focus of both scholars and tourists for a long time. But most laymen associate them first with Mayans and Aztecs. They have indeed built some of the most breathtaking pieces, but as with many other things, they have only perfected something that the Olmecs have started. One of the earliest and biggest pyramids, at least at the time of building, is found at La Venta. It is actually seen as the center structure for the whole settlement. Today, after 2,500 years of erosion, the only thing left from it is a mound as it was built from clay that has a slightly conical shape At first, it made archeologists think it was purposely built that way to mimic the nearby mountains. But the recent studies have shown that they were similar to the pyramids of their successors. When it was still in its original form, it was a proper rectangular pyramid with stepped sides and inset corners. Being 34 meters (110 feet) high, it was the biggest building in that settlement, and maybe even of the whole Olmec world. That is why archeologists have aptly named it "The Great Pyramid."

The actual use of the pyramids in the Olmec civilization is still debated. At one side of the debate stand the scholars who think that these pyramids are temples, as were the Mayan and Aztecan pyramids. They think the Olmecs built them to be closer to the sky and the gods when performing religious rituals and ceremonies. On the other side of the debate, the less popular theory suggests that they were tombs, like those in ancient Egypt. Evidence that supports this is the fact that a magnetometer survey found an anomaly deep beneath an estimated 100,000 cubic meters (3.5 million cubic feet) of earth that fills The Great Pyramid. They speculate it could be a resting place of an important ruler. Another piece of supporting evidence to this theory is the fact that archeologists have found burial mounds with similar shapes which are seen as precursors to the pyramids. Though that may be true, the question remains—why would a tomb be the center focus of the whole city? Some researchers explain the anomaly as merely an unintentional byproduct of the building process or an offering built on the foundation of the temple to please the gods. Whatever may be the true function of the pyramids in Olmec society, the fact remains that they were among the first ones to build them, and through their influence, they were crucial in spreading them across the region.

What is left of the Great pyramid at La Venta.

The pyramids are now pretty much gone from the Mesoamerican cultures. But another Olmec innovation was so intertwined with everyday life that it's traces could be connected with the fact that one of the most popular sports in this region is football (soccer). That shouldn't be surprising considering that in the pre-Columbian era they played a Mesoamerican ballgame, which is quite similar to football, and whose earliest traces could be found on Olmec sites. The game was played in almost every civilization of Mesoamerica, but with the rules and exact details varying from culture to culture and from time period to time period. Even today, in certain areas of Mexico, people still play a game called Ulama, which came from the Aztec version of the game. The universal characteristic to all variations of the game was the rubber ball it was played with, though they varied in size. The oldest rubber balls came from El Manatí, a settlement close to San Lorenzo. These balls were dated to around 1600 BCE. Other evidence also corroborates this idea, like the number of ballplayer figurines found at San Lorenzo, from 1200 BCE. The fact that the balls were found in a sacrificial bog and that near it archeologists found a "yoke", which is a statue in the form of the upside-down letter U, made out of stone. That is usually connected to the Mesoamerican ballgame, led scholars to conclude that these balls weren't just a sacrificial offering. Rather, they think the game was played near the site in a form of a religious ritual of some sorts.

The evidence found in the cultures that came after the Olmecs confirm that the game was both religious in nature and recreational. It was an essential part of city life, usually played on special courts built only for the game. And while the significance of this game in the social life of the region is undoubtful, there is a major debate about another aspect of it. It is regarding the possibility of the human sacrifice being the part of the Mesoamerican ballgame. It is commonly considered that in the Mayan society the game ended with the losing side, or at least its captain, being ritually killed. Some theories even link this with the game being used to settle municipal grievances and inter-city conflicts. But so far, no such evidence has been found at the Olmec sites, leading scholars to believe that they played a more peaceful version of the game. Yet, its religious symbolism and importance in the Olmec society is certain. But how exactly it was connected to their beliefs is still under question. As it was played with two teams competing against each other, some see it as a ritual representation of the struggle of the day and night or life and underworld. Others concluded that the ball represent either the sun, which is more likely, or the moon. And the scoring hoops, through which the ball was supposed to be passed through for a point, was hypothesized to have represented equinoxes, sunrises, or sunsets. The last possible connection is fertility, as some of the ballplayer figurines of the period were found adorned with maize symbols. And some of those figurines seem to be representations of women. Both of these are often connected to fertility in the Olmec world, as well as other Mesoamerican cultures.

There is another cultural innovation that is surely connected with fertility, and that is the Mesoamerican Long Count calendar, popularly known as the Mayan calendar. The most striking characteristic of that calendar is that it revolves around the cycles. The shortest cycle is K'in, a single day, while most measures stop at the fifth cycle, B'ak'tun, which is approximately 394 years long. Interestingly, the longest cycle found is a ninth one, named Alautun, which is a bit longer than sixty-three thousand years. That cyclical nature of the Mesoamerican calendar made a lot of people believe that an end of a cycle meant the end of the world, which led to the 2012 media frenzy about the apocalypse. Of course, that faulty idea of the world ending came after an incorrect interpretation of an ancient Mayan text which mentioned that an old world ends and a new arises, meaning a new cycle starts after the end of the thirteenth B'ak'tun which ended on December 21st, 2012. On the other hand, the starting point of this calendar is 3114 BCE when translated to our calendar. Because of that it is considered that the Mesoamericans believed the world in which they lived was created at that date. But at this point, it should be noted that this calendar was not of Mayan creation; it was used across the whole region, and several archeological findings connected to the Mesoamerican Long Count calendar predates the Mayans by several centuries. And some of the earliest discoveries are connected with the Olmecs.

One of the oldest calendars was found at the Tres Zapotes site, which is located in the Olmec heartland and was at one point a part of the Olmec civilization. But it is also one of the few larger settlements that outlived the Olmec civilization as we see it today. The calendar found at that site is dated roughly to 32 BCE, which predates the rise of the Mayans by at least 300 years. But as it was found at the settlement which was at one point part of the Olmec culture, some see it as a direct connection with that civilization. Two other calendars of the same age have been found on the Guatemalan Pacific Coast and in the southern Mexican state of Chiapas. Both of them are similar in age to the one found at Tres Zapotes. Their link with the Olmecs is more indirect. These calendars were decorated in the Olmec style, not the Mayan, but were also in many other aspects far away from the Olmecs. The biggest problem with this theory of the Mesoamerican calendar being of Olmec origins is the fact that all these calendars were created about 300 years after the Olmec civilization had withered away, but that isn't the final nail in the coffin for it, as there could be some older calendars that still haven't been found. And their indirect ties to the Olmec are unquestionable. Looking at other important innovations and cultural advancements that came from this civilization, combined with this circumstantial evidence, it is not that unlikely that it was the Olmecs who first created the calendar, or at least created the foundation for it. But so far, most scholars tend to leave the question of the Mesoamerican calendar origin open until more concrete evidence is found.

The Mesoamerican calendar seems quite odd to most people nowadays because most people are used to the base 10 counting system, otherwise known as the decimal system, which is used in all measuring systems today. On the other hand, the Mesoamericans used base 20 in mathematics. The exception for that is the third cycle, which was 360 days long, and was based on the number 18, most likely so it would be roughly the length of a solar year. But one of the more interesting facts connected with the Long Count calendar is the usage of zero. That number is generally considered to be an essential step in cultural and scientific development as it is a sign of developed intellectual thought and also has a practical application in many fields of life. When the Mesoamericans needed to represent the absence of a number, they used a shell-like glyph, which in its essence was a symbol for nothing, mathematically speaking a zero. The Mesoamerican invention of zero happened at least few hundred years before the Arabs and Hindus. And if we connect the invention of the Long Count calendar with the Olmecs, then they could become the first to use a concept of zero. Of course, this claim is directly linked to the debate over if the Mesoamerican calendar was indeed an Olmec calendar.

Another heated debate over the contributions of the Olmecs is if they had developed writing, which is considered instrumental in forming a successful civilization. A stone tablet found near San Lorenzo, named the Cascajal Block, contains 62 glyphs. Some of these symbols resemble maize, pineapples, insects, and fish, while others seem to be more abstract, as they look like boxes and blobs. This, for some scholars, clearly represents a writing system, even if it was rudimentary. And as it was dated between 1100 and 900 BCE, it shows that the Olmecs had achieved basic literacy much earlier than others in Mesoamerica, with the oldest non-Olmec writing being dated to around 500 BCE. But as with all other aspects of the Olmec civilization, this is also a debated topic. For some archeologists, these symbols are too unorganized, without much similarities to other Mesoamerican writing systems. So rather than an example of writing, they suggest these glyphs may have individual meaning and are not mutually connected in a higher meaning. And if they are not connected, then they are just a compilation of symbols, not a written language. And some of them are similar to the symbols found on some pieces of Olmec art where they have been described as purely decorative. This could also indicate that the Cascajal Block could have some ornamental function rather than a practical use of relaying a message. But even if these glyphs are not a clearly developed writing system, it would at least indicate a formation of it.

Another piece of archeological evidence found at the San Andrés, a settlement near La Venta, is a much clearer sign that the Olmecs had their own writing system. Three artifacts, out of which a ceramic cylinder seal is the most important, were dated to 650 BCE, which is still about 150 years older than the oldest currently confirmed Mesoamerican writing. The seal contains three glyphs when combined in a way which the later Mesoamericans, most notably the Mayans, commonly used to represent a name of the ruler. Besides the seal, two small greenstone plaques have been found, both with only one (different) symbol each. But both of these symbols have been connected to well-documented glyphs in other Mesoamerican writing systems, again most notably the Mayan scripts. For the archeologists that agree with the theory of Olmec script existing, this is clear evidence of it, which when connected with the Cascajal Block, give a sense of continuity and development of the Olmec writing system. When compared with the traditions of the Mayan writing system, it indicates that the Olmec script no matter how rudimentary it may have been, has been the base on which all other Mesoamerican civilizations built their own writings. This would be another testament to the importance of the Olmecs in the development of the whole Mesoamerican region.

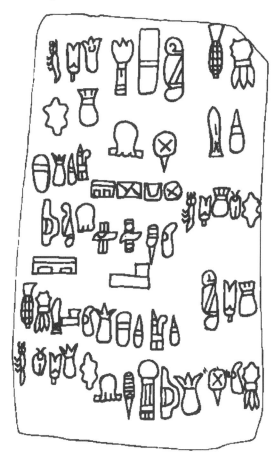

A drawing of the Cascajal Block

Presently, one of the most iconic foods linked with Mexico and the Mesoamerican region is tortillas, primarily the ones made out of maize. That type of food has been made in this area since before the

Spaniards came, who actually gave it the name we call it now, since tortilla in Spanish means a small cake. In the Aztecan Nahuatl language, it is called tlaxcalli, which means something baked. We can't be sure what the Olmecs called it, but we know they made it. The evidence for this lies in archeological findings of comales, ceramic griddles on which tortillas were traditionally cooked. The interesting thing is that there weren't any comales found at the San Lorenzo site. But at La Venta, comales have been found, although they were not that common in the Olmec heartland. But like many other things, they were more commonly found at the Olmec-influenced sites. This means it was likely that both comales and tortillas had been developed in the later period of the Olmec civilization. Of course, this doesn't prove anything conclusively; they may have used those ceramic griddles for preparing other types of food and that those have been later adapted for making tortillas.

On the other hand, although traditionally tortillas have been made on comales, in some earlier forms they could have been made in some other way, which would suggest that tortillas could be older than the Olmecs. But even if they didn't invent the tortillas they could have perfected the way they were made. Clearly, tortillas played an important role in the development of Mesoamerica. At first glance, some people may see it as just food, without any further implications other than gastronomical culture. Tortillas have an advantage of staying fresh and edible for at least several days. Also, they were prepared and transported fairly easily. That would have improved the military and travel logistics of the Olmecs, making longer trips easier to organize and execute. In that way, tortillas may have been crucial for even the expansion of the Olmec trade network in the La Venta period, making it larger and more complex than before. And because the Olmec traders would almost certainly bring them on their travels, we can conclude they also spread it across Mesoamerica, making it a popular food in the region. So, even if they didn't invent or even improve tortillas, it is likely the Olmecs played a crucial role in spreading its use to other Mesoamerican civilizations.

While on the subject of culinary history, talking about Mesoamerica and not mentioning cacao and its usage would be a huge oversight. Cacao was an essential part of all Mesoamerican cultures, with a wide variety of application in everyday life. They made various types of beverages from it, used it in religious ceremonies, and at some points during the history of the region, it was used as currency as well. And the use of the cacao bean dates back all the way to the Olmec times. Evidence for that lies in the vessels found at various Olmec settlements, which after testing showed traces of cacao residue in them. This would confirm that the Olmecs drank one of the variations of the cacao beverages, which would put their civilization into the contest of being the first one to actually do so. The fact that the cacao tree grows naturally in the Olmec heartland also helps the case. It was only a matter of time before someone would think of some way to use its fruit.

From the vessels found, scholars are sure that at least one of the ways the Olmecs used cacao was to make drinks out of it. But some also think they used it in more spiritual and ceremonial ways, linking it from the very beginning of its usage to religion, as it was used in later Mesoamerican civilizations, but archeologists can't be sure about that. The third common usage of cacao as a currency seems rather unlikely for the Olmecs. Not only is there no evidence of cacao being used as one, but also, there is no evidence of a currency of any kind being used, although the Olmecs have traded with and for cacao, and its use as currency in later periods of Mesoamerican history rose from that trade. The biggest testimony to the crucial role the Olmecs played in making cacao a special part of Mesoamerican culture lies in the very word cacao. The word we use today is a Spanish transcription of Mayan word cacaw, which was their name for the cacao. But the Mayans got the word from the Olmec language, where this plant was called kakaw, according to the work of Mesoamerican linguists. That alone is enough to imply how important the Olmecs were to the spreading of cacao and its use over the region. But also looking at the bigger picture; it shows that this civilization didn't influence only the Mesoamerican civilizations, but that they with this word managed to influence the worldwide culture of the present era, as we even today love and use cacao, while still using the Olmec name for it. And other examples in this chapter also support the idea that the Olmec influence was much more widespread than they are usually credited for.

Chapter 11 – The Olmecs, A Mother Culture of Mesoamerica?

In this book, even from its title, the point has been in celebrating the Olmecs as one of the oldest, if not the oldest, civilization in Mesoamerica. And throughout the pages, the general tendency of the chapters has been to present all the ways in which the Olmecs have influenced both their contemporaries and their successors. Even when considering the theories that were against this notion, the idea that the Olmec civilization is a mother culture of all Mesoamerica should be obvious. And many scholars agree with this, though in various degrees. But there are also those who are completely against it. And this chapter is dedicated to the negative side of this important debate, as the positive side has been woven into all the previous chapters.

Looking at the Olmecs as a mother culture of the region, the religion seems to be the part where the Olmecs influence is the weakest. In previous chapters, it has been mentioned that their beliefs influenced others enough to pay respect to both Olmec holy sites and to at least some of their gods. Some scholars, however, believe it is also possible that these religious beliefs weren't solely Olmecan. It is possible that they actually predate the Olmecs. These beliefs could have come from the prehistoric Mesoamericans, who due to the fact that they lived in the same regions, started worshipping the same supernatural beings and animals, attributing to them similar connections to the natural phenomena in an attempt to explain them. With continued contact among the different tribes, their beliefs became more alike to the point when they became almost the same. In this sense, some scholars believe the religion and mythology of Mesoamerica didn't evolve from the Olmec beliefs and were instead merely one of many bricks in the wall.

And, as we have seen, a lot of their art stemmed from their religion. So, the issue regarding the cultural and artistic influence the Olmecs had on Mesoamerica through the times is also open for debate. As mentioned in previous chapters, the consensus among historians is that the Olmecs' style was copied by other chiefdoms and civilizations, spreading the characteristics of the Olmec culture across the region But contrary to that idea, some scholars think this explanation of mimicry is wrong. As with religion, they think that these similarities in art, which most have seen as copying of the Olmec style, are rooted in the cultural unity of the entire region, which predates the Olmecs. They think that nearly all of the people who lived in Mesoamerica had the similar aesthetics as well as beliefs, and without foreign influence made art with only minor, almost indistinguishable differences. That would mean that the Olmec style didn't exist. It was, in essence, a style of the entire Mesoamerica. If that's true, it would certainly make the Olmecs less special in the eyes of scholars, at least when talking about art.

Even when talking about the Olmecan cultural innovations mentioned in the previous chapter, theory is similar – they were created by the entire region, not only the Olmecs. There is no clear evidence that the Olmecs were first to make any cultural advancements. The oldest evidence for any of them have been dated to a similar age, and not all of them came directly from the Olmecs. This brings the question; did the Olmecs influence Mesoamerica? Or did Mesoamerica influence the Olmecs similar to the old conundrum of the chicken and the egg? While it is possible the Olmecs were actually the ones to make these innovations, it is also possible they copied them from their neighbors or trading partners. It is even possible that similar ideas on how to improve the quality of life were created in different tribes and chiefdoms without the Olmecs' influence. And with that mindset, they cannot be called the Mesoamerican mother civilization.

Some of the scholars even argue that the Olmecs weren't more advanced than any of their contemporaries and that they were more or less equal to other cultures of Mesoamerica at the time. They do not stand out in art, craftsmanship, or social complexity. The only thing that separates them from other tribes is their trade and their wealth. With all that being said, it could be concluded that the Olmecs were only a creation of modern times, a group of people that we linked into a civilization that wasn't as tangible as we would like it to be. And that in reality all the tribes and people of the region were actually unified in one widespread ancient Mesoamerican civilization. Of course, this is just another way of looking at the Olmecs and shouldn't necessarily be taken as the correct one. This debate is still not completely settled.

Conclusion

The Olmec story is filled with maybes, debates, theories, and ideas. With all these unanswered questions, the Olmecs are still largely a mystery to us. The Olmecs played an essential role in Mesoamerican history; from the beginning of their history, they started to stand out from their neighbors. They were able to create amazing temples, monuments, and other public projects. They had the finesse to create astonishing pieces of art of unparalleled quality for the time period. They were able to create a society which strived for more, which strived for greatness. And because of their excellence, the Olmecs served as a model to others around them at the time. That is why everyone tried to copy their ingenuity and why everyone wanted to be associated with them.

Of course, this doesn't mean that their society was perfect, nor their civilization a place where one would actually want to live. It should always be remembered that the majority of the Olmec people, the commoners, led hardworking lives, with very little leisure and luxury. The Olmecs shouldn't be viewed as some past utopia in any way. But even so, it was exactly these commoners who managed to achieve such proficiency in many diverse fields of work. They became the famous artisans whose products are still the focus of public attention. But with so many uncertainties and debates, some may ask if the Olmecs really deserve the hype that has been built up around them. Has the web of legend been spun around them only because they are one of the oldest civilizations of the Americas?

If nothing else, they deserve our attention because of the trade network they created, which in the end seems to be not only the core reason for their success, but also their greatest legacy. The Olmecs' influence and power stems from the fact that they had unprecedentedly capable merchants. With all the connections they had across the whole of Mesoamerica, they made the region feel much smaller, more linked, and more compact. This is possibly their greatest achievement. What didn't originate from them, they helped spread. So even if we can't or won't give the Olmecs the title of the Mesoamerican mother culture, we can't ignore the fact that they were important for the development of the region. They were the glue that stuck it all together in the first place.

For that reason, their story deserves to be told. That is why it is worth our time and patience to get to know the Olmecs. It is important to see them as artists and craftsmen, as warriors and rulers, as traders and priests, as shamans and inventors. Because even if their civilization is long gone and they have disappeared in dark corridors of the almost forgotten past, the Olmecs' have put their mark on history. Their impact can still be felt today, even if it is in a minor, almost unrecognizable way. And that fact should never be forgotten.

Preview of Maya Civilization

A Captivating Guide to Maya History and Maya Mythology

Introduction

You've probably heard of the Maya and their astounding civilization before. You may recognize the famous Maya calendar that apparently predicted a worldwide apocalypse back in 2012. The media were quick to jump on board this mind-boggling prophecy (which we'll debunk later in this book). Newspapers and websites were filled with stories of doomsday that failed to materialize. Lucky for us, we did wake up on December 22, 2012, when the Maya calendar apparently ended.

But what you may not know is how much the Maya legacy is impacting your life today. Do you love to treat yourself to a frothy hot chocolate before bed, or indulge in an after-dinner chocolate treat? Do you love adding a side of fries to your meal? What about tomatoes for your favorite Italian dishes? If you do, you may not be aware that you have the Maya and the Spanish conquistadors to thank, for they introduced these goods to Europe and other continents.

But Maya are far more than just their food. In this captivating guide, you'll discover why Maya have gained such worldwide admiration over the many other civilizations that existed in Mesoamerica at the time. You'll learn how the Maya civilization developed, the major turning points in their 3,000-year-long history, the mysteries surrounding their demise, and some of the unique places where Maya exist to this day.

Oh yes. If you think the Maya are gone, think again. As opposed to popular belief, the Maya are neither extinct, nor quiet. They are six-million strong, according to some sources, most of them living in Guatemala. What's more, in 1994 one of the surviving Maya tribes, the Zapatistas, launched a rebellion in southeast Mexico against global trade and capitalism.

In the first part of this book, we'll first examine the origins of the Maya civilization and the Mesoamerican cultures that may have influenced them. We'll discuss why Maya (out of all the different tribes that existed in the region at the time) have captured the imagination of the West so much. We'll look at how they lived, ate, slept, whom they worshipped, and how they used herbal medicines and hallucinogenic plants to treat the sick.

We'll look at their trading routes and rivalries with another famous Mesoamerican tribe—the Aztecs. We'll look into the decline of the Maya civilization and how their rivalries with the Aztecs aided the victory of the Spanish conquistadors in the 16th century, led by the famous Spaniard Hernán Cortés. We won't forget to mention the heroic efforts of the Maya to fend off the Spaniards, and why they were able to succeed at this task for much longer than the Aztecs. We'll even track down the Maya living today, a population that is still six-million strong and adhere to many of the traditions that their ancestors once held. In among the battle tales and gore of human sacrifice, we'll look at some delicious cocoa recipes, Maya-style, that you can make at home.

After we've learnt all about the Maya origins, their cuisine, and their most notable events to present day, we'll delve into the aspect that's often the reason why so many people have been fascinated by the Maya civilization throughout the ages. We will look at their mythology, cosmology, and the solar calendar that resulted in the infamous doomsday scare back in 2012.

So buckle up and get ready to be transported to the warm and wet plains of the Maya civilization—it will be a journey you'll never forget.

Maya Timeline

The Archaic Period:

- 7000 to 2000 BC

The Preclassic Period:

- Early Preclassic – 2000 to 1000 BC
- Middle Preclassic – 1000 to 300 BC
- Late Preclassic – 300 BC to AD 250

The Classic Period:

- Early Classic – AD 250 to 600
- Late Classic – AD 600 to 900
- Terminal Classic – AD 900 to 1000

The Postclassic Period:

- Early Postclassic – AD 1000 to 1250
- Late Postclassic – AD 1250 to 1521
- The Spanish Invasion – AD 1521

Glossary of Important Maya Terms

- Cacao – the seeds that the Maya used in order to create their delicious cacao drink, also known as "bitter water."
- Cenote – a type of sink-hole that the Maya used to get fresh supplies of water (and to perform ritual sacrifice).
- Conquistadors – the Spanish military leaders who led the conquest of America in the 16th century, including Hernándo Cortés.
- The Dresden Codex – located in a museum in Germany, the Dresden Codex is one of the oldest surviving books from the Americas. It contains 78 pages with important information on rituals, calculations, and the planetary movements of Venus.

- Haab – one of the several Maya calendars (this one measured time in 365-day cycles).
- Hero Twins – the central characters in the Maya creation story and the ancestors of future Maya rulers.
- Huipil – traditional dress for Maya women.
- Maize – the staple food of Maya civilization, an ancient form of corn (the Maize god was one of the most important deities for Maya).
- Mesoamerica – this is what we call the region of the Americas before the arrival of the Spanish fleets and its colonisation in the 15th and 16th centuries.
- Popol Vuh – the story of creation of the world that was passed down from generation to generation (it was recorded by the Quiche Maya who lived in the region of modern day Guatemala).
- Shamanism – an important spiritual practice throughout Mesoamerica (during shamanic trance a shaman would be able to practice divination and healing).
- Stelae – an upright stone slab or column, often used as a gravestone. These structures usually contained commemorative inscriptions.
- Yucatan Peninsula – a region in the southeast of Mexico, where some of the Maya civilization developed, especially in the Postclassic period.

Part 1 – History

Chapter 1: The Origins of the Mesoamerican Civilizations

Maya have captivated the imagination of the West ever since their culture was "discovered" in the 1840s by the American writer and explorer John Lloyd Stephens and the English artist and architect Frederick Catherwood. The latter is best known for his intricate and detailed images of the Maya ruins that he and Stephens later published in their book *Incidents of Travel in Central America*.

But just because the West didn't discover the Maya until the mid-nineteenth century doesn't mean that they lived in obscurity the rest of the time. In fact, their history is rich with fantastical tales and splendour and a diet that people living in other regions at the time could only dream about. The origins of the Maya civilization can be traced all the way back to 7,000 BC.

The Archaic period: 7000 – 2000 BC

People were once hunter-gatherers, living a largely nomadic lifestyle, according to the whims of nature and the sharp-toothed animals all around them. They had to keep moving in order to stay safe and keep up their food supplies. But in 7000 BC a new shift began—the hunter-gatherers who lived in Mesoamerica discovered something that would change their region forever. They began planting crops.

It's not entirely clear why this shift occurred when it did. The changing weather patterns may have had something to do with it— the climate gradually became wetter and warmer, so many of the larger animals that the Mesoamericans relied on for food became extinct. As a result, they had to eat more plants and grains, so eventually they started growing some for themselves. They used many techniques to make their lands more fertile. For example, they discovered that burning trees helped put nitrates into the soil to make it more fertile. (Don't try this at home.)

As a result, these ancient people started having a much more varied diet. We know this thanks to the discoveries by the archaeologists working in the Tehuacan Valley of Mexico, a site that contains the best evidence for human activity in the Archaic time period in Mesoamerica. The locals were able to plant and eat things that we often take for granted today, such as peppers, squash, and avocado. Not to mention early forms of corn, the grain that would become the staple food in Mesoamerica.

Since they were able to grow the food that they needed in order to survive, these ancient people no longer needed to move around as much. They began settling down into small villages, leading to the first known settlements in Mesoamerica. The first evidence of individual burial spots directly under people's homes dates back to 2600 BC. These early settlements included temples and sacred spots for worship, suggesting an early form of a civilization. Temples, worship, and sacrifice remained a prominent theme throughout the Maya history, and we'll cover more of it later.

But the Maya did not evolve in a vacuum. There were many cultures and tribes that existed around them, and each had some influence on their culture, customs, and civilization. We'll examine these, one at a time, as we travel through time to really appreciate the interplay between those cultures and the Maya. Before we go onto learning about how these early settlements evolved into the Maya civilization, let's look at one of the most important tribes that existed in Mesoamerica at the time—the Olmecs.

The Olmecs: 1,200 – 300 BC

No one really knows where the Olmecs came from or where they disappeared to. But their legacy on the Mesoamerican tribes, including the Maya, is huge.

The Olmecs inhabited the area along the Gulf of Mexico, and their impressive stone cities gave way to myths about giants who may have lived in this area at the time. The Olmec craftsmanship was highly sophisticated—there are some impressive sculptures that survive to this day as evidence of their superb skills.

Sometimes ancient history is a bit of guesswork, leaving you to fill in the gaps left out by missing evidence. It's interesting that there's a total lack of battle scenes in the Olmec art—something that most other cultures are quick to display in their monuments and sculptures. The fact that they depict no battle scenes could mean one of two things. Either they did not engage in any war conflict, or they simply didn't feel like showing off about it. You decide.

Until recently, the Olmecs were regarded as the "mother culture" of all the great Mesoamerican civilizations to come, including the Maya and the Aztecs. But more recent sources argue that the Maya actually had a counter-influence on the Olmecs.

When it comes to the Olmec mythology, displayed in their surviving temples and sculptures, there are definite traces of shamanic practice. Many of their sculptures depict a were-jaguar, a core element of shamanism, symbolizing shamanic trance. The Maya saw the jaguar as a transformational animal, who feels at home at night-time, a symbol for the Underworld. The symbolism of shamanistic practice is present in all later Mesoamerican cultures, including the Maya.

The Olmecs may have had an important motif of a twin deity, that may have influenced the mythology of the Maya Hero Twins. The Hero Twins is a way to express the duality that the Maya saw around them—the complementary duality between day and night, life and death, the masculine and the feminine. The Olmec flaming eyebrows, the first corn, and cross bands are all symbols that would later appear in the Maya art, connected to astrology. Ancestor worship was also prevalent in the Olmec tradition, as it was later in the Maya and most Mesoamerican cultures at the time.

Challenge your perceptions—Dwarfism

When studying ancient history and learning about cultures, it's always interesting to find out what light it can shed on the culture that we inhabit today. Sometimes the things that we perceive as true are to do with our cultural upbringing. For example, nowadays we define people who are born with smaller organisms and don't grow much taller than 147cm as having the medical condition of Dwarfism or "short stature." We tend to see this as an abnormality, assuming that people born with this condition would face certain limitations in life.

Well, the Olmec also saw Dwarfism as an abnormality, only not a limiting one. In fact, it was quite the opposite. As the director of the Maya Exploration Center, Dr. Edwin Barnhart explains in his audio-lecture series *Maya To Aztec: Ancient Mesoamerica Revealed* that if you were born with a very small organism in the Olmec or the later Maya culture, you'd be seen as a magical being, touched by the gods. You'd be enjoying all kinds of luxuries, often appearing in the king's court. This may be something to do with their belief that the sky was held up by four dwarves, and so they gave them special treatment.

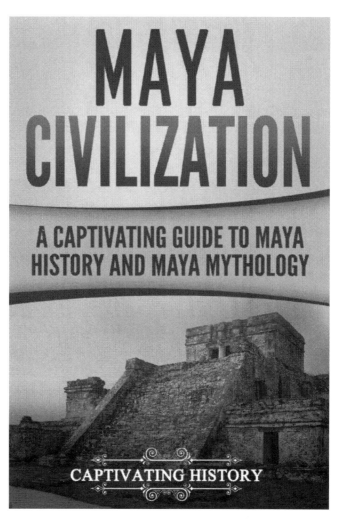

Check out this book!

Preview of Aztec

A Captivating Guide to Aztec History and the Triple Alliance of Tenochtitlan, Tetzcoco, and Tlacopan

Introduction

Nothing remains of the ancient Mesoamerican civilization who called themselves the Mexica, better known to us as the Aztecs. Nothing except for their remarkable story.

In this book, we discuss their enigmatic origins and how the Aztecs rose from nomadic tribes to the dominant power in Mesoamerica at an astounding speed. You'll wander the streets of their great capital city of Tenochtitlán, known as "the Venice of the New World" among the Spanish Conquistadors, who spread the term all over Europe. You'll discover the full extent of the city's splendour, visiting its many market stalls, smelling fresh chocolate and vanilla pods. You'll indulge in a taste of ripe, hand-picked avocados and freshly baked corn tortillas, as you decipher Náhuatl, the language spoken by the 50,000 merchants who visited Tenochtitlán every day.

You'll probably wonder how this great city, built in the middle of a lake and isolated by two of Mexico's highest mountains, Iztaccihuatl and Popocatepetl, could ever be defeated. From the arrival of the first Spaniards in 1519 to the eventual fall of the Aztec empire, we'll talk you through the major battles that eventually led to its fall. We'll uncover lies and deceptions in the alliance with their neighbouring cities of Tetzcoco and Tlacopan. We'll also look at Aztec legacy on the world today: how Tenochtitlán became the basis for the capital of the New World and evolved into today's Mexico City.

Remember the most interesting stories are peppered with fascinating contrasts and paradoxes. Perhaps this is what makes the Aztecs so interesting. They emulated and idolized the Toltec civilization in everything they did, although there's no archeological evidence to support that the great Toltec civilization even existed. Each year, the Aztecs performed a substantial number of brutal human sacrifices, yet they were also completely devoted to intellectual pursuits, such as mathematics, public speaking, and the arts.

Masters of their own fate, the Aztecs re-wrote their story of origin, burning their history books. This has enmeshed much of their history with mythology and made it difficult to separate myth from fact. Further complications were caused by the Spanish conquistadors and their successors, who wanted to portray themselves in a good light or justify their conquest when writing their accounts of the Aztecs.

Chapter 1 – The Origins of Aztecs: A Tribe Destined for Greatness

On the Mexican flag backdrop of a vertical tricolour of green, white, and red, a fierce eagle sits on top of a cactus plant, wrestling with a snake that it's snatched in its mouth. This is the symbol of the Aztec city of Tenochtitlán and tells the story of how a humble tribe from the North, who called themselves the Mexica, rose to astonishing wealth and power just a few hundred years after finding their 'promised land,' known today as Mexico City.

Let's look at the origins of the Mexica civilization, better known to us by the name of the Aztecs.

Rewriting Aztec history

The story of their origin is obscured by legend. The Aztecs arrived and settled in the Valley of Mexico around the year 1250 AD, and they most likely came from the North. Thanks to a tyrannical move by one of their kings, Itzcoatl, who ruled the Aztec empire from 1427 to 1440, all the books that told the story of Aztec history up to that point were burned.

The son of a slave woman and a nobleman, Itzcoatl quickly rose to power, thanks to his military achievements. He was set for greatness, and, perhaps to erase his heritage of being born to a slave woman, he made earnest efforts to rewrite the history of the Aztecs to create a more palatable version of their origins.

Another book-burning incident took place much later, destroying more crucial information about the Aztecs. It was done to heavily censor the Florentine Codex, a 12-volume work by the Franciscan monk Bernardino de Sahagún. He spent years interviewing the local tribes, learning about the ancient Aztec language of Náhuatl and their many rites and customs. When he returned to Europe in 1585, the Spanish authorities confiscated much of his original material, destroying this valuable resource. The later versions of the Florentine Codex that did get published were most likely heavily censored, erasing many captivating details that would have shed light on the Aztecs and other ancient Mesoamerican cultures.

Because of these unfortunate instances, what we know of the origins of the Aztec civilization are draped in myth, and subject to much speculation by archaeologists and historians.

Aztlán - the cradle of Aztec civilization

Aztlán is a bit like Atlantis, a legendary ancient land that disappeared and has puzzled researchers for years. Even the Aztecs were fascinated with finding the mystical land of Aztlán. Similar to King Arthur's mission to find the Holy Grail, the Aztec ruler Montezuma I gathered his fiercest warriors and most knowledgeable scholars in the 1450s and sent them on a mission to find Aztlán. Apparently, they succeeded, although the maps they drew have not survived, so their success remains debatable. It was said to be located somewhere to the north of Tenochtitlán, and, like the Aztecs' great city, Aztlán too was in the middle of a lake.

While it could be nothing more than Aztec propaganda to depict an idealized version of their origins and to support their claim of rulership, the myth of Aztlán is fascinating. It was incredibly important to the Aztecs too - the term Aztec means "the people of Aztlán." Although the Aztecs called themselves the Mexica, they did regard themselves as the direct descendants of the tribe that used to live in Aztlán.

The myth of Aztlán

When the Spanish arrived in Mexico in the 16th century, they became fascinated by the Aztec culture. They made several attempts to document their origin story, and parts of it were recorded by Diego Duran, a Dominican friar who arrived in the New World in 1540 when he was five years old. A document called *Los Anales de Tlatelolco* (The Annals of Tlatelolco), now held at the National Library of France in Paris, also reveals much about the lost land of Aztlán.

These accounts reveal the fascinating story of Aztlán and the origins of the Aztec civilization. Translated, the word "Aztlán" stands for "the place of white birds" or "the place of herons." According to legend, the Aztec emerged from the hollow earth through a system of caves, along with six other tribes (Acolhua, Chalca, Tepaneca, Tlahuica, Tlaxcalan, and Xochimilca).

A depiction of Chicomoztoc — the place of the seven caves. Source: https://en.wikipedia.org/wiki/Aztl%C3%A1n

The seven tribes wandered the Earth together, sometime between the years of 1100 and 1300. Then the other tribes decided to migrate south while the Aztecs remained in the north. They eventually found their "paradise," called Aztlán. It was a large island in the middle of lake Metztliapan ("the lake of the Moon").

The science of linguistics can help trace the true origins of Aztlán. The Aztec language of Náhuatl comes from the Uto-Aztecan language tree. Robert Bitto explores this further in his podcast *Journey to Aztlán, the Mythical Homeland of the Aztecs*. He explains that several tribes who lived to the north of Mexico spoke a language that belonged to the same language tree. Along with some indigenous tribes from northern Mexico, these include the Hopi, the Pima, and the Utes of Utah, USA. The linguistic connection stretches as far as Idaho and Montana, supporting the claim the Aztecs did come from the north. Scholars agree the most likely location for Aztlán is in the northern or central parts of Mexico.

Considering that Aztlán was as good as paradise, why did the Aztecs decide to leave?

The fall of Aztlán

Some accounts state the Aztecs fled because they were encroached upon by a tyrannical ruling elite that wanted them expelled or enslaved. Once they began to flee, they were pushed further and further south by the Chichimecas, a warlike marauding tribe.

Other accounts state there was a natural disaster of such a magnitude it drove the Aztecs out of the area and forced them to migrate south. Climatic studies conducted in the region support this claim, stating that between the years of 1100 and 1300 a mass migration occurred to the south-west of the modern-day United States. This was most likely because of a lengthy period of drought. The Aztecs left the area around 1200 AD, so this theory is plausible.

After leaving Aztlán, the Aztecs became a nomadic tribe, wandering the plains of northern Mexico, and making their way south for two hundred years. They endured many hardships along the way before they eventually settled on the tiny island in the middle of Lake Texcoco in the Valley of Mexico, where they founded their great city of Tenochtitlán. According to legend, the Aztecs were guided and seen through their hardships by a deity called Huitzilopochtli, the Aztec god of war, the sun, and human sacrifice. He was later the patron god of the city of Tenochtitlán.

But it wasn't a straight journey, and by no means easy either. The Aztecs made several stops along the way, even settling temporarily in some of these areas. At times, some of the Aztecs wanted to remain and began opposing the priests who urged them to keep moving. Battles broke out amidst their own people, as they wandered the land for nearly two hundred years, from hardship to hardship. Until they finally arrived in the Valley of Mexico. But the welcome they received wasn't quite what they'd expected.

Chapter 2 – The Unwelcome Arrival in Mexico Valley

After two hundred years of exile, the Aztec was on a quest to find a new homeland. They had finally reached the Valley of Mexico, where their priests had guided them and instructed them to settle. However, they were not welcomed by the locals, who were wary of foreigners. Their journey had been hard, but life was not about to get any easier for the Aztecs.

They arrived in the Valley of Mexico around the year 1300 AD. The valley was bustling with various tribes and civilizations, most of them rivals. Professor Edwin Barnhart explains what happened to the Aztecs after they arrived in Mexico Valley and before they founded their great capital of Tenochtitlán in chapter 33 of his lecture series *Maya to Aztec: Ancient Mesoamerica Revealed*. According to him, the Aztecs were "outnumbered, outranked, and outclassed," a stark contrast to the bustling civilization the Spaniards found just over 200 years later.

Two of these rival tribes were larger than the rest - the Tepanecs and the Culhuacan. The Tepanecs allowed the Aztecs to settle, granting them Chapultepec or "the grasshopper hill." It was situated on the west shore of Lake Texcoco, now the central park of Mexico City. Their subway system also features icons relating back to this period - one of the stops is depicted as a hill with an ant on it, symbolizing the grasshopper hill.

The Tepanecs were a dominant force in the area, taking over after the Toltec empire fell around 1200 AD. Many cultures around the time, including the Aztecs, went to great lengths to claim themselves as descendants of the ancient Toltec civilization and to emulate their achievements. However, the Toltec civilization may have never existed at all.

Settling in Chapultepec

It wasn't long before the Teponecs grew annoyed with the Aztecs. Less than a year later, they kicked them out. At this point in history, the Aztecs acted like savages. They didn't pay their tributes to the Tepanecs, and were considered uncultured savages.

The Aztecs fled Chapultepec and travelled south. They reached the area controlled by the Culhuacan, who granted the Aztecs a barren land known as Tizapan. It was infertile and impossible to farm. The Aztec diet consisted mainly of lizards and rodents.

But their god Huitzilipochtli was never far from them, at least according to the Aztec priests who provided guidance. They said the Aztecs should take up deeds that honoured the war god and do the 'dirty work' that no one else wanted to do. This helped the Aztecs to develop a sophisticated warrior culture.

This tactic paid off. Twenty years later, the Aztecs had intermarried with the people of Culhuacan and their children were immersed in their culture. After more than two hundred years of unrest, things were finally looking up for the Aztecs, until one fatal day that changed everything.

Sacrifice gone wrong

It's important to understand the meaning of human sacrifice for the Aztecs. They believed sacrifice was a welcome offering to their gods, and many people gladly engaged in acts of self-mutilation. Sacrifice was often a way to get closer to the gods, so when Achicometl, the ruler of Culhuacan, offered his daughter to the Aztecs for marriage in 1323, they thought it would be a better idea to sacrifice her to their gods. In turn, this would make the king's daughter into a goddess.

Except Achicometl did not see it that way. One day, he saw one of the Aztec priests wearing the flayed skin of his daughter during a festival dinner. Far from thanking the Aztecs for their attempt to make his daughter into a deity, he was so horrified he cast them out. Somewhat confused, the Aztecs were forced to wander the Valley of Mexico once more.

The vision of their new home

One day, as they wandered around Lake Texcoco to find their new home, their high priest had a vision. "Our promised land will be marked by an eagle, sat on a cactus, holding a snake in its mouth," he announced, coming out of his trance. The Aztecs didn't have their own land yet, but at least they had a sign of what they were looking for.

Hopeful, they settled with the Teponecs once again. Having learned their lesson, the Aztecs paid tribute to the Teponecs and fought for them. They added more problems in the valley where several tribes and cultures were already fighting each other. They fought against Culhuacan while searching for the sacred sign that would mark their new home.

Two years later, their priest finally saw the sign. Huitzilipochtli certainly wasn't giving them an easy time - their promised land was in the middle of a lake on a tiny island. Shallow, marshy land made up the island, but the Aztecs followed their god and settled there. In 1325, the Aztecs began to build Tenochtitlán on the island. Little did they know that a hundred years later the Aztecs would dominate the entire region, and this tiny island would become one of the greatest cities that Mesoamerica had ever seen.

Building a city on a lake

The land that the Aztecs found was just a tiny island, surrounded by a lake. They employed a local farming method called *chinampa.* They created artificial islands in the lake by piling up mud and soil in the shallow lake bed. These islands looked like small, rectangular areas where the Aztecs could grow crops. According to Jorge, M et al., these measured at 30 m × 2.5 m and the Aztecs measured these beds in *matl* (one *matl* was equivalent to 1.67 m). First, they marked the limits of the soil bed by using stakes they pushed into the shallow lake bed. Next, they fenced it off in a rectangle, using a lightweight construction material called wattle. They made it by weaving thin branches together and tying them to upright stakes to form a woven lattice.

This was demanding work, but it paid off because the soil was incredibly fertile for planting crops. Although they were still paying tribute to the Tepanecs, in time, they could live on their land autonomously and grow crops. What's more, the area was defensible because it was perched in the middle of a lake and surrounded by water.

Life was still tough for the Aztecs. Jose Luis de Rojas, an anthropologist from the University of Madrid, wrote that "early years were difficult." People lived in huts, and even the temples dedicated to Huitzilopochtli were made of "perishable material." But day-by-day, their territory expanded until in 1325 they named their new city Tenochtitlán.

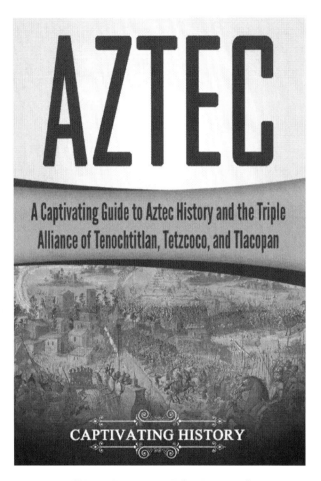

Check out this book!

Bibliography

Adams Richard E. W. and MacLeod Murdo J., *The Cambridge history of the native peoples of the Americas Volume II: Mesoamerica*, Cambridge, Cambridge University Press, 2008.

Carmack R.M., Gasco J. and Gossen G.H., *The Legacy of Mesoamerica: History and Culture of a Native American Civilization*, New York, Routledge, 2007.

Coe Michael D. and Koontz Rex, *Mexico – From the Olmecs to the Aztecs,* London, Thames and Hudson, 2013.

Bernal Ignacio, *The Olmec world* , Berkley, University of California Press, 1969.

Hassig Ross, *War and Society in Ancient Mesoamerica*, Berkley, University of California Press, 1992.

Koontz R., Reese-Taylor K. and Headrick A., *Landscape and power in ancient Mesoamerica*, Boulder , Westview Press, 2001.

Pool Christopher, *Olmec Archeology and Early Mesoamerica*, Cambridge, Cambridge University Press, 2007.

Staller John E. and Carrasco Michael, *Pre-Columbian Foodways: Interdisciplinary Approaches to Food, Culture, and Markets in Ancient Mesoamerica*, New York, Springer, 2010.

Rosenswig Robert M., *The Beginnings of Mesoamerican Civilization: Inter-regional interactions and the Olmecs*, Cambridge, Cambridge University Press, 2010.

The Olmec and Toltec: The history of early Mesoamerica's most influential cultures, by Charles Rivers Editors, 2016.

Free Bonus from Captivating History (Available for a Limited time)

Hi History Lovers!

Now you have a chance to join our exclusive history list so you can get your first history ebook for free as well as discounts and a potential to get more history books for free! Simply visit the link below to join.

Captivatinghistory.com/ebook

Also, make sure to follow us on:

Twitter: @Captivhistory

Facebook: Captivating History:@captivatinghistory

Made in the USA
Columbia, SC
12 January 2019